COOKING WITH
BEER
IN COLORADO

COOKING WITH
BEER
IN COLORADO

75 COLLABORATIVE RECIPES
WITH FORT COLLINS' BEST CHEFS AND BREWERS

CHRISTINA MARIE
Photography by Tim O'Hara

Published in 2015 by Chefs on the Go
www.chefsonthego.com

Printed in Canada

Library of Congress Control Number: 2015918535

ISBN: 978-0-9969708-0-8

Editor: Brian Kittrell
Art Direction & Design: René Larson
Design & Production: Jenny Fischer
Photographer: Tim O'Hara

www.cookingwithbeerincolorado.com

THIS BOOK IS DEDICATED TO MY FORT COLLINS CHEF AND BREWER FAMILY.
YOU ARE MY INSPIRATION.

A HEART OF GRATITUDE

To the talented chefs and brewers of Fort Collins: Mission accomplished! 14 brewers, 31 chefs, and 75 recipes later, this book has become a reality because of you! I think we can all tip our hats and jump for joy after reflecting on this exquisite adventure. I couldn't ask for a better group of passionate chefs and brewers to work with for the making of this book—you are the dream team! Thank you for joining me in this journey, sharing your stories, and for the gift of your time in creating the most innovative beer recipes known to man! My heart is filled with the utmost respect and I owe a great deal of gratitude to each of you. This book clearly wouldn't exist without you!

Tim O'Hara, how did I end up with the most adored photographer in the whole wide world? It's definitely worth mentioning a little thanks to the lovely Stefanie O'Neil who led me to your talent! I'm so grateful for your magnificent photos; this book would not look as "beertiful" without your pictures! You have captured the essence of this book in every shot—shooting the sweetest moments between the brewers and chefs along with their yummy dishes and brews! Each photo shoot was an absolute blast. Here's to more sushi dropping on the floor during future shoots. Sorry, but you are stuck with me and I'm never letting you go!

To Brian Kittrell, I'm so appreciative for your endless hours of edits, for your patience, and for being my sounding board! To René Larson and Jenny Fischer, you both are extremely talented designers. Thank you for bringing my vision to life, for your time, and for your fabulous designs.

To Joseph O'Leary, my mentor and friend, thank you for helping me move forward with this idea, and for your guidance and belief in me. To Toby Naad, thank you for teaching me about the art of publishing. Thanks to Jenny Roemer and Jonson Chatterley for proofreading this beast.

To my mother and brother, thanks for your infinite love and encouragement. Finally, to my nana and papa—you are truly the best grandparents and the reason I am where I am today. I love you so much!

Christina Marie

CONTENTS

FOREWORD

Crafty brews and tasty foods are the perfect ingredients for a successful recipe! Luckily I live in Fort Collins, the "Napa Valley of Beer," and Front Range playground with more restaurants per capita than any other city in Colorado. The heart of this community is the chefs and brewers that make it so unique and delicious. If you have spent any time in Fort Collins you will quickly discover it is not your typical city—you will most likely fall in love and stay forever.

Part of what makes this place so special is how it is centered on building relationships and collaboration. It's not unusual for brewers to come together and develop a beer, or for chefs to brainstorm with each other to stir up their next dish. I have been blessed to get to know these kind and innovative masterminds, and am eager to share their creativity.

Cooking with Beer in Colorado is a collection of 75 collaborative recipes from 31 chefs and 14 brewers in Fort Collins. However, this is much more than your typical cookbook. This book is about people and their own unique personalities. I invite you to experiment with these downright delectable recipes and read the stories along the way. The recipes are written in the chefs' own words, and the brewer's notes are prepared by the brewers themselves to show off their personal styles.

I hope this book will inspire you to build relationships in your own community, as well as discover the joys of collaboration and cooking with beer! In my humble opinion, these recipes are beerlicious masterpieces! So fill your growler and prep your palette, as you are about to partake in an exquisite cooking adventure. By all means, sip on that tasty beer you're cooking with because that's half the fun!

Cheers!

ODELL BREWING COMPANY

established 1989

Jeff Doyle ODELL BREWING COMPANY

Brandon Hocke SPOONS - SOUP, SALAD AND SANDWICHES

TR Shuttleworth SONNY LUBICK STEAKHOUSE

David McKissick THE BOOT GRILL

ODELL BREWING COMPANY COLLABORATIONS

JEFF DOYLE, ODELL BREWING COMPANY

If you look closely behind the beer tank in the group picture on the right, you'll see a life-size poster of Jeff wearing cut off jeans and rocking out on an electric guitar. This epitomizes his fun and fearless character known to light up the brewery. "No one pays money for angry beer," laughs Jeff. He was introduced to brewing while attending art school and working as a part time prep-cook at Granite City Food and Brewery in St. Cloud, Minnesota. Jeff grew vastly as a brewer when his craft brewing curiosities led him to an apprenticeship at Odell Brewing Company. "I knew I had a solid foundation when I gathered 100 people to drive to the middle of nowhere for a kegger with my new beer creation. I appreciate what I do. I never knew I would be so valued." Now the Assistant Brewer at Odell, he eagerly experiments with beers—rarely making the same recipe twice. Currently on tap is his Cocoa Kolsch, a chocolate concept beer he made with local cocoa nibs and husks from Nuance Chocolate. "I tried to keep it as light as possible while maintaining the chocolate aromas from the cocoa husks." Jeff continues to challenge himself to make his beer, and life, zesty, vivacious, and always fun.

BRANDON HOCKE, SPOONS - SOUP, SALAD AND SANDWICHES

According to Brandon, a sense of community was instilled in him from a young age. "I grew up on a ranch in Salida, Colorado and saw the whole food chain process and community behind it. On chicken butcher day, my family and two others gathered together on my family's farm. The moms plucked the feathers in the kitchen, and the dads chopped their heads off in the barn," says Brandon. Since then, he's strived to incorporate this community-oriented approach as a chef at Spoons - Soup, Salad and Sandwiches. For example, every Saturday, he and a few of the restaurant employees visit Fossil Creek Farm to handpick fresh organic vegetables, which they then incorporate into their dishes. "Going to the farm supports our Spoons community, local businesses, and allows us to serve something we are proud of." In 2006, Brandon graduated from CSU with a degree in History, and made the decision to begin a culinary career. He received his professional training at the five star hotel and restaurant, Greenbrier Resorts in Virginia. He found that he loved Fort Collins, and returned to become the general manager of Spoons. During the weekends, he manages to bike to at least one brewery in Fort Collins, as well as spend time in his garden. "I spend my quiet time in my yard—which is a disaster. That should tell you how much free time I have."

ODELL BREWING COMPANY COLLABORATIONS

T.R. SHUTTLEWORTH, SONNY LUBICK STEAKHOUSE

T.R. traces his love for cooking to his favorite childhood memory of learning to make a sautéed lemon chicken pasta from his mother. As an only child raised by a single mother, T.R. assumed the role of household chef in an effort to contribute to the family. This experience led him to discover his passion for cooking. "I love making pretty things and putting them down on a plate to make someone smile." Thirsting for travel and adventure, T.R. opted out of culinary school, studied with prestigious chefs in five different states, then met and married the love of his life. The newlyweds honeymooned to Fort Collins, and decided to settle down. In the kitchen, T.R. enjoys expressing his artistic side through creating "food sculptures." "Artistic outlet is necessary for my brain. I love plate presentation and creating sculptures—like stacking mac & cheese on top of short ribs. It's kind of fun. I make little sculptures everyday and watch people destroy them." Outside of his signature sculptures, he enjoys spending time with his family, hiking, biking, and camping in the woods.

DAVID MCKISSICK, THE BOOT GRILL

David McKissick, found a way to combine his love for eating and the outdoors through cooking. "Sometimes, I would see what vegetables were growing in our garden, catch some fish, and then throw them on the grill." David went to college in Hawaii and followed in his father's footsteps to study Marine Biology. During his studies he continued to get in tune with his inner chef. "I cooked extravagant dinners for my roommates, and the occasional date. I had some positive reviews from them, and surprised myself with how good the meals turned out. I discovered I was more passionate about cooking than Marine Biology," says David. This led to his move to Fort Collins where he earned a degree in Business that would enhance his understanding of how restaurants are run. After completing his degree, David decided to pursue cooking full force. As a chef, he finds pleasure in passing his cooking knowledge onto others. "I love tying in my own culinary creative flair with education." With a desire to inspire, David often participates in culinary outreach in the community by leading various cooking demonstrations at Crescendo, a quaint local spice shop. David's latest hobbies are reliving his childhood memories by cooking with fresh vegetables from his backyard and hosting BBQ parties at his house.

GREEN CHILE CHEDDAR SOUP WITH 90 SHILLING ALE

COLLABORATION	**ODELL BREWING COMPANY** Brewer, Jeff Doyle
	SPOONS - SOUP, SALAD AND SANDWICHES Chef, Brandon Hocke

PREP TIME: 30-45 minutes
4-6 SERVINGS (10 OUNCE)

1	tablespoon cooking oil	¼	cup mild green chiles
½	cup sweet onion, diced	¼	cup hot green chiles
½	cup celery, diced	¼	cup heavy whipping cream
1	teaspoon garlic, minced	2	cups shredded cheddar cheese
1½	tablespoons chili seasoning	¼	cup corn starch
2	teaspoons cumin	4	tablespoons water
1	bottle Odell 90 Shilling Ale		salt and pepper
2	cups vegetable stock		

Heat oil in a four-quart pot and sauté onions and celery until onions begin to turn translucent. Add garlic and sauté for one to two minutes. Add chili seasoning and cumin. Cook for one minute. Measure ¼ cup of beer, pour into pot, and scrape the bottom of the pot with wooden spoon. Add vegetable stock and green chiles, bringing the soup to a simmer. Pour in heavy cream. Keeping soup at a very low simmer, slowly add cheddar cheese, stirring the entire time. Add remainder of beer and allow soup to slowly simmer for five to 10 minutes, continuing to periodically stir. Mix together water and corn starch to form a slurry. Slowly add to soup, stirring constantly to reach desired thickness. Salt and pepper to taste.

CHEF'S NOTE: Be sure to keep the soup at a simmer. Boiling will allow the soup to lose liquid, curdle the cheese, or possibly burn. Yes, you can burn soup!

BREWER'S PAIRING: Odell 5 Barrel
5 Barrel is my go to beer. It's a well-balanced English style pale ale but fits the style with a dry finish, which cuts the richness of a cheddar based soup.

SPOONS CUTTHROAT PORTER CHILI

COLLABORATION | **ODELL BREWING COMPANY** Brewer, Jeff Doyle
SPOONS — SOUP, SALAD AND SANDWICHES Chef, Brandon Hocke

PREP TIME: 1 hour
8-10 SERVINGS

2	tablespoons cooking oil	¼	teaspoon black pepper
¾	pound pork, diced	¼	teaspoon dried oregano
¾	pound beef, diced	½	teaspoon ground cumin
1	cup onion, diced	4	teaspoons chili seasoning (use your favorite)
2	cups peppers, diced (use a mixture of your favorites. Anaheim, bell, jalapeño, cubanelle, ancho, hatch, etc.)	2	tablespoons tomato paste
5	cloves garlic, minced	1	large lime, juiced
1	bottle Odell Cutthroat Porter	1½	cups water
3	(15.5 ounce) can diced tomato	2	tablespoons fresh cilantro, chopped
1	(14.5 ounce) can beef broth	2	(15 ounce) cans beans, drained and rinsed (use your favorite)
1	ounce Mexican chocolate		sea salt
3	tablespoons canned chipotle in adobo sauce, minced		

Pour oil into a two-gallon stockpot. Sear meat until beginning to brown, and season with a sprinkle of sea salt, black pepper and chili seasoning. Continue to sauté briefly so the meat picks up the chili flavor, and then add all the vegetables. Add the Cutthroat Porter and allow to simmer for five minutes. Add all the remaining ingredients EXCEPT the beans, cilantro and sea salt. Simmer your chili until the meat is tender and the liquid has reduced (30 minutes). Add the beans, cilantro and sea salt (to taste).

CHEF'S NOTE: Chili is always better the next day, so if you can resist, chill overnight. As with anything you cook, always adjust the seasoning to your liking at the end of the cooking process.

BREWER'S PAIRING: Odell Levity Ale
Dark kilned barley of a porter lends a strong roasted note to the chili itself and Levity Ale is a deliciously quaffable golden amber to quench the fire of a green chili tongue.

"ARTISTIC OUTLET IS NECESSARY FOR MY BRAIN. I LOVE PLATE PRESENTATION AND CREATING SCULPTURES—LIKE STACKING MAC & CHEESE ON TOP OF SHORT RIBS. IT'S KIND OF FUN. I MAKE LITTLE SCULPTURES EVERYDAY AND WATCH PEOPLE DESTROY THEM."

- T.R. SHUTTLEWORTH

LEVITY BRAISED BEEF SHORT RIBS

COLLABORATION	**ODELL BREWING COMPANY** Brewer, Jeff Doyle
	SONNY LUBICK STEAKHOUSE Chef, T.R. Shuttleworth

PREP TIME: 30 minutes
6-8 SERVINGS

2-3	tablespoons blended oil		2	cups leeks, sliced
5	pounds beef short ribs		1	tablespoon peppercorns
½	gallon veal stock		4	bay leaves
2	cups red wine			salt and pepper
12	ounces tomato paste			green onions, chopped
2	bottles Odell Levity Amber Ale			

Liberally salt and pepper the ribs on all sides. Heat the oil in a heavy bottom pot. Work in batches, searing the ribs on all sides, then transfer to a deep roasting pan. When all of the ribs are seared, add the leeks and wine to the pot. Loosen all of the browned bits from pot then add the mixture to the pan with the ribs. Add the rest of the ingredients except the green onions to the ribs, cover with aluminum foil and place in a 300° oven for six hours or until the meat is very tender and falling apart. Remove the ribs from the liquid and set aside. Transfer the liquid to a pot and simmer until sauce has reduced and thickened. Season with salt and pepper and then strain. Replace the ribs into the sauce and serve. Garnish with some chopped green onions.

CHEF'S NOTE: Serve with some sautéed hearty greens like kale or mustard greens and fried Easy Street Wheat Mac and Cheese.

BREWER'S PAIRING: Odell Runoff Red IPA
The red color comes from a malty backbone and complements a hearty red meat dish. The acidity of hops in an IPA works as a tenderizer for the meat itself and lends a floral fruity accent to the peppercorns and leeks.

EASY STREET WHEAT MAC AND CHEESE

COLLABORATION | **ODELL BREWING COMPANY** Brewer, Jeff Doyle
SONNY LUBICK STEAKHOUSE Chef, T.R. Shuttleworth

PREP TIME: 45 minutes
8 SERVINGS

2	pounds cooked pasta		1	quart milk
½	cup yellow onion, diced		½	bottle Odell Easy Street Wheat
¼	cup unsalted butter		2	cups smoked cheddar, shredded
¼	cup flour			salt and pepper

Cook pasta and cool. Sauté the onion in butter until translucent then add flour to the butter and whisk together. Continue to cook roux for five minutes on low heat. Add the beer and milk and stir to avoid clumping. Heat on low until mixture becomes thick, and then add cheese and pasta.

CHEF'S NOTE: Try cooling mac and cheese in a large dish and cut it into squares. Then dredge in flour, egg wash and bread crumbs. Place in deep fryer until golden brown.

BREWER'S PAIRING: Odell Easy Street
An unfiltered wheat beer works best, as the yeast plays off the starchy aspect of the macaroni. Wheat beer, like mac and cheese, is an historic craft staple evoking the fundamentals of soul food. The drinkability of wheat beer almost matches the versatility of mac and cheese. Each can be a meal in itself.

DESSERT WELLINGTON

COLLABORATION | **ODELL BREWING COMPANY** Brewer, Jeff Doyle   **THE BOOT GRILL** Chef, David McKissick

PREP TIME: 1 hour
BAKE TIME: 30 minutes
12 SERVINGS (1 INCH PIECES)

1	(5 pound) bag of frozen mixed berries	1	pound cream cheese (room temperature)
2	cups sugar		
1	bottle Odell Loose Leaf	1	10x2" slice of cake (can be store bought sheet cake, I prefer white or vanilla)
	puff pastry 12" x 12"		

MIXED BERRY COMPOTE: In a saucepot combine berries, two cups of sugar, half a bottle of Loose Leaf, and let simmer (continue stirring, breaking up berry pieces). Sauce should reduce then cool in fridge.

ASSEMBLING THE ROLL: Lay out puff pastry on a lightly dusted cutting board, brush the egg wash on the edges of the puff pastry. In the center of the puff pastry place some of the berry compote in a straight line to match the length of the cake slice. Place dollops of cream cheese every inch on top of the berry compote. Then, place the cake loaf on top of the compote and cream cheese, and repeat with another layer of compote and cream cheese. Roll the puff pastry into a burrito and crimp the two joining sides together. Ensure crimp is nice and tight. Flip whole log over so crimped side is on bottom. Next crimp the ends with a fork and make sure they are tight. Place on a nonstick sheet tray and put four two-inch slits in top so steam can vent out. Then brush with egg wash and sprinkle sugar over top. Place in 350° oven until top is golden brown.

DESSERT WELLINGTON GARNISHES

PREP TIME: 30 minutes

1	pint heavy whipping cream	1	bag of milk chocolate chips
1	teaspoon lemon juice	2	tablespoons of salted butter
1	pinch of salt	1	bottle Odell Cutthroat Porter
2	cups sugar	½	cup heavy cream
1	bottle Odell IPA		

WHIPPED CREAM: In a stainless steel bowl add heavy whipping cream, lemon juice, salt and sugar. Either whisk by hand, or use a mixer. Mix until all ingredients incorporate, then add half a bottle of Odell IPA and continue mixing. Whip until mixture starts to get nice peaks.

CHOCOLATE SAUCE: In a double boiler add chocolate chips, butter, and cream. Continue to stir, ensuring ingredients do not get too hot and separate. Once mixture is smooth, add in half a bottle of Odell Cutthroat Porter. Remove from heat and stir until incorporated.

CHEF'S NOTE: If you prefer to complement rather than contrast a dessert, choose a fruited style that is still respected in the craft community. Friek "fruited sour style" is an amalgamation of the words Frambroise, and Kriek, which translate to raspberries and cherries. Brewed in the style of a Belgium Lambic ale, it could also be substituted with a sour beer. Sour beers were long ignored in American Craft Brewing as the wild yeasts were seen as a technical flaw, but within the last few years they have regained recognition for their historical value and they are among the fastest growing trends in the craft beer industry. Raspberries, cherries, and dessert—need I say more? Once you taste it, you'll know.

BREWER'S PAIRING: Odell Runoff Red

There's something about the complexity of this dessert. There are so many elements involved. The necessity of harmony amongst the many elements of the dessert requires equivalence in beer pairing. Runoff Red is a red IPA that gets its color from deeply caramelized malts and as an IPA holds hops heavy-handedly.

SUPPLY

COOPERSMITH'S PUB & BREWING

established 1989

Dwight Hall COOPERSMITH'S PUB & BREWING

Chris O'Mara COOPERSMITH'S PUB & BREWING

Eric Lu LULU ASIAN BISTRO

COOPERSMITH'S PUB & BREWING

COOPERSMITH'S PUB & BREWING
and LULU ASIAN BISTRO

DWIGHT HALL, COOPERSMITH'S PUB & BREWING

In 1989, Dwight helped open the first brewpub and longest established brewery in Fort Collins, Coopersmith's Pub & Brewing, located in the heart of Old Town Square. Initially working in the kitchen, he transferred to the brewing scene when the original head brewer requested his assistance. Dwight explains, "I always liked beer, I stumbled upon it. My detail oriented and relaxed personality was a good fit for brewing." From there, he progressed as a brewer and took over the brewery in 1997. Since then, he has contributed to over 150 innovative beer recipes including his famous spicy Sidga's Green Chili Ale. Not only is Dwight a talented brewer, he is also an avid mountain biker and skier, and appreciates his bonding time with his children on the slopes. He expresses a heart of gratitude to be a part of the brewery scene, "I'm the luckiest guy in the world to do what I do—I make craft beer in Fort Collins, and am super fortunate."

CHRIS O'MARA, COOPERSMITH'S PUB & BREWING

"Life is short, enjoy what you do, and do what you love. That's my motto, and I try to abide by it daily," explains Chris. From humble beginnings in the restaurant industry as a line cook, he eventually worked his way up to part owner at Coopersmith's Pub & Brewing. Chris's passion for beer and food fit well into the pub/brewery concept. He loves the family feel and having the freedom to develop new recipes. For example, his creamy Chocolate Challah Bread Pudding has been on the menu for 10 years now and is the most popular dessert. He also finds great delight in cooking with beer. "Everything is a little better with beer and we often try to incorporate it into our menu items to enhance the flavor." To add a little kick to his dishes, he will occasionally cook with his signature Coopersmith's Sidga's Green Chili Ale, or combine his brews with local meats such as his hearty Lamb Highland Horsetooth Stout Cottage Pie. After a long day in the kitchen, you may find Chris riding his motorcycle and getting lost in the back roads of the mountains.

ERIC LU, LULU ASIAN BISTRO

Steeped in culinary tradition, Chef Eric Lu knows the meaning of his Asian roots, and how it translates into his adored restaurant, Lulu Asian Bistro. According to Eric, he grew up in the food business. "I was raised in China, where Asian cuisine was a central part of my family. My parents owned a Chinese restaurant, and I learned from them and was able to use my own culinary creativity." When he was 19 years old, he left China with a dream to open his very own restaurant in America. Eric's dream became a reality when he started a Mexican restaurant in New York City followed by a Japanese restaurant in Las Vegas. While living in Vegas, he visited a friend in Fort Collins and was introduced to his next bistro destination. "My friend showed me Old Town and I told myself, one day I will have a restaurant here. It seemed to be great timing, as Asian restaurants were scarce in Fort Collins then." In 2007, Eric established Lulu Asian Bistro and offers a selection of his own Asian creations along with his family's traditional secret recipes. He brings a taste of Asia to you, not only in his delicious dishes, but also in his cozy atmosphere. You can gaze at his beautiful paintings imported directly from China or dream about being a ninja as you look at his warrior sculptures dispersed throughout the restaurant. On a nice Sunday afternoon, Eric loves to have a cold beer and fish at Horsetooth Reservoir. If you're looking for the full Lulu experience, make sure to try a sake bomb. Eric will most likely join in the fun and pour you a drink you will never forget.

HIGHLAND HORSETOOTH STOUT COTTAGE PIE

COLLABORATION | **COOPERSMITH'S PUB & BREWING** Brewer, Dwight Hall   Chef, Chris O'Mara

PREP TIME: 1 hour
9 SERVINGS

1	pre-made pie dough		1	celery stalk, diced
4	pounds mashed potatoes		1	teaspoon pepper
			1	teaspoon garlic
FILLING			2	quarts lamb stock
2½	pounds lamb meat, cubed		¼	cup tomato paste
1	tablespoon rosemary			
3	bay leaves		**ROUX INGREDIENTS**	
2	teaspoons salt		½	pound of butter
¼	cup Coopersmith's Horsetooth Stout			flour to thicken
2	large carrots, diced			

Place all filling ingredients in large pan and cook over medium heat until vegetables are soft. Then cool. Create roux by melting ½ pound of butter in a saucer, stir in flour until mixture is thick like a paste. Transfer liquid to sauce pan and thicken with roux, this will be your gravy.

Take pie dough (your favorite recipe will do or use a pre-made one), roll out and place into a 13" x 9" baking pan. First, spread two pounds mashed potatoes onto pie dough, then your lamb and vegetables, and finish with remaining mashed potatoes. Cover with foil and bake for 45 minutes at 450°. Remove foil, bake another 15 minutes to brown. Let stand for 10 minutes, cut into nine servings and top with your lamb gravy and Parmesan cheese. We serve ours with homemade warm applesauce.

CHEF'S NOTE: Be sure to let the pie sit for 10-15 minutes to firm up, this will help when cutting to hold its shape.

BREWER'S PAIRING: Coopersmith's Poudre Pale Ale
The crisp malt and hop flavors of the Poudre Pale Ale are a nice balance to the rich lamb and Parmesan flavors in the Highland Cottage Pie.

"EVERYTHING IS A LITTLE BETTER WITH BEER AND WE OFTEN TRY AND INCORPORATE IT INTO OUR MENU ITEMS TO ENHANCE THE FLAVOR."

- CHRIS O'MARA

HORSETOOH STOUT BEER BREAD

COLLABORATION	COOPERSMITH'S PUB & BREWING
	Brewer, Dwight Hall Chef, Chris O'Mara

PREP TIME: 1½ hours
2 LOAVES

4½	teaspoons bread yeast
2	cups white rye flour
4½	cups all purpose flour
2	teaspoons salt
1½	cups warm water
¾	cup Coopersmith's Horsetooth Stout
½	cup molasses
2	tablespoons oil

Combine all dry ingredients in a mixing bowl. Combine wet ingredients in separate mixing bowl. Stir liquids into the flour mixture, then knead dough until smooth and elastic, place into greased bowl, cover and let rise in a warm place until it doubles in size. Knead again, then split dough into equal parts and place into two 9" x 5" x 2" greased loaf pans. Let it rise again about an hour. Place into 400° oven uncovered for 25-30 minutes. Cool bread on a wire rack, and then serve with honey butter.

CHEF'S NOTE: This beer bread goes perfectly with a hearty soup.

BREWER'S PAIRING: Coopersmith's Not Brown Ale
The sweet molasses flavor of the bread is complemented by the roasted malt in the Not Brown Ale.

HORSETOOH STOUT ICE CREAM FLOAT

COLLABORATION	COOPERSMITH'S PUB & BREWING
	Brewer, Dwight Hall Chef, Chris O'Mara

2	scoops vanilla ice cream
	Horsetooth Stout Beer to taste

Drop two scoops vanilla ice cream in a pint glass, top with Horsetooth Stout Beer and enjoy!

KOLSCH THAI CHICKEN BASIL

COLLABORATION | **COOPERSMITH'S PUB & BREWING** Brewer, Dwight Hall   **LULU ASIAN BISTRO** Chef, Eric Lu

PREP TIME: 1½ hours
2 SERVINGS

1	chicken breast
1	egg
2	tablespoons vegetable oil
1	teaspoon cornstarch
½	green bell pepper
½	red bell pepper
2	cups of Shitake mushrooms sliced in halves
1	cup of cherry tomatoes
1	green onion, cut into ¼ inch lengths
1	teaspoon jalapeños sliced

½	teaspoon of ginger or to desired taste
1	cup of loosely packed fresh basil leaves

SAUCE:

1	teaspoon sugar
½	teaspoon salt
1	teaspoon fish sauce
1	teaspoon chicken flavored powder
1	cup water
1	cup Coopersmith's Columbine Kolsch

1 Slice chicken and marinate with water and salt for one hour.

2 Once the chicken is marinated, mix in an egg, cornstarch and vegetable oil.

3 Bring water to boil in wok, and add chicken.

4 Once chicken is cooked, drain water completely.

5 Again, bring water to a boil in wok, then add bell peppers, mushrooms, cherry tomatoes, green onions, jalapeños, ginger, and basil leaves. Stir-fry chicken until almost cooked.

6 Drain water and set aside.

SAUCE:

7 Heat up wok with vegetable oil. When it is hot, add sugar, salt, fish sauce, chicken flavored powder, water and beer.

8 When it is well mixed add all vegetables and chicken.

9 Serve!

CHEF'S NOTE: Make sure to drain all water from dish and not to add too much, otherwise it will make a soup.

BREWER'S PAIRING: Coopersmith's Columbine Kolsch
The bright malt flavors of the Columbine Kolsch complement the light fresh flavors of the Thai Chicken Basil.

PANANG CURRY

COLLABORATION | **COOPERSMITH'S PUB & BREWING** Brewer, Dwight Hall **LULU ASIAN BISTRO** Chef, Eric Lu

PREP TIME: 1½ hours
SERVES 2

1	chicken breast		½	cup snow peas
1	egg			
1	teaspoon cornstarch		**CURRY SAUCE:**	
2	tablespoons vegetable oil		2	tablespoon of Panang curry paste
1	cup of Shitake mushrooms sliced in halves		1	cup coconut milk
1	small deep-fried diced potato		1	cup of Coopersmith's Sigda's Green Chili
½	cup yellow diced onions		1	teaspoon sugar
½	green bell pepper		¼	teaspoon salt
½	red bell pepper			

1 Slice chicken and marinate with water and salt for one hour.

2 Once the chicken is marinated, mix in an egg, cornstarch and vegetable oil.

3 Bring water to a boil in wok, then add chicken.

4 Once chicken is cooked, drain water completely.

5 Again, bring water to a boil in wok. Add in mushrooms, potato, onions, bell peppers, snow peas and chicken. Only cook until almost cooked.

6 Drain water and set aside.

FOR THE SAUCE:

7 Heat up wok with vegetable oil. Put in Panang curry paste, then add in the coconut milk, beer, sugar and salt.

8 When it is well mixed add the vegetables and chicken.

9 Serve!

CHEF'S NOTE: The sauce can be thick, so only heat the sauce on a medium level and keep stirring otherwise you could burn it.

BREWER'S PAIRING: Coopersmith's Sigda's Green Chili Beer
The spicy kick of the Sigda's Green Chili Beer is a natural match for the spiciness of the curry.

NEW BELGIUM BREWING COMPANY

established 1991

Grady Hull NEW BELGIUM BREWING COMPANY

Ricky Myers JAX FISH HOUSE

Jeff Nanbara JAWS SUSHI

NEW BELGIUM BREWING COMPANY COLLABORATIONS

GRADY HULL, NEW BELGIUM BREWING COMPANY

New Belgium's well-respected brewer, Grady Hull, is guaranteed to give you a great laugh and a fun educational beer experience. He is also likely to leave you with a jolly heart and quite possibly a little tipsy. Grady is a firm believer that a case of bad events can turn into good happenings. A series of these events occurred for Grady, which in turn shaped his career as a brewer at New Belgium Brewing. The first incident occurred after he totaled his Datsun 240. His friend that helped him with his recovery happened to introduce him to his new favorite hobby, home brewing. This led to an immediate change of major to Food Science, which allowed him to focus on the sensory aspect of brewing. Post graduation, he was turned down from a brewery he wanted to work for, however a better position soon presented itself. "I was really bummed that I didn't get the job, but that's why I applied for the Coors sensory job. That experience in their sensory lab is what eventually led me to me getting my dream job here at New Belgium. They wanted someone to start a sensory program." Grady is now living the dream as a brewer and loves every day at work. "It's a fun club to be a part of, and for that I consider myself very lucky." When he isn't brewing, he is often riding bikes with his two children.

RICKY MYERS, JAX FISH HOUSE

Cruising around on a bicycle at New Belgium Brewery while holding a plate of his Snap Shot Braised Beet Salad, Chef Ricky Myers gives you a glimpse of his playful personality. Originally from Atlanta, Georgia, Ricky's love for the mountains guided him to Colorado, where he began his culinary career. He started his training at The Art Institute of Denver, which led to opportunities such as working as a chef in private jets, and being a part of the Wolfgang team. "I loved the mountains, so I cooked and snowboarded my way around Colorado." Currently working at Jax Fish House in Fort Collins, Ricky likes the challenge and creativity of being a chef. "I love the ability to learn something new everyday—it's never boring." He will occasionally get in tune with his southern roots and create dishes that are seriously soulful such as his Lager Lobster Po' Boy. Ricky also enjoys featuring local dishes and incorporates the community as often as he can. "The food scene in Fort Collins is all about collaborating and being locally sourced. The chefs and farmers in the community recognize in order to build a food scene, we have to work together." The close ties he has with local farmers, allows him to plan specials that are based on what they can offer him. For example, the ingredients in his Garden Sweet Strawberry Salad, are sourced locally including the honey used in his vinaigrette from Copoco Honey. He also did a spin on a clam chowder called the Fort Collins Style Chowder because he would rotate local beers into the chowder. Ricky's main outlet from cooking is playing guitar or biking with his wife and enjoying some local beers. He also has a soft heart for his dog, Pepper Anne.

JEFF NANBARA, JAWS SUSHI

Jeff began his career as a sushi master at a Fort Collins staple, Suehiro. He remained there for 16 years, and eventually had a desire to branch out and start his own sushi restaurant. As a result, Jeff and his two friends Adam and Will established JAWS to showcase their love of sushi and drinking. Jeff explains, "Our main focus is having fun! We often watch Kung Fu movies on our projector, listen to a wide variety of music, and create cool dishes such as The Agent Orange Roll, complete with crushed Cheetos on top." The atmosphere is always enjoyable and you'll be sure to hear 'KOBAYASHI' yelled loud and clear when you leave the restaurant (an expression that doesn't necessarily mean anything, and refers to Takeru Kobayashi, a Japanese hot dog competitive eater). Jeff is known to keep things interesting not only with his creative sushi dishes, but also with his fluctuating hairstyles. His partner in crime and co-worker Zach explains, "You never know what color hair or cut Jeff will have next. When he started JAWS it was blonde and now it's a Mohawk." Jeff is also an avid Broncos fan and enjoys spending time watching their games. Don't be surprised if you find Jeff in the stadium cheering on his favorite team with bright orange and blue hair.

SNAP SHOT BRAISED BEET SALAD

| COLLABORATION | **NEW BELGIUM BREWING COMPANY** Brewer, Grady Hull |
| | **JAX FISH HOUSE** Chef, Ricky Myers |

PREP TIME: 1½ hours
SERVES 2

BEETS

2	medium sized beets, tops removed	¼	cup sugar
1	orange, halved	1	tablespoon salt
4	sprigs of fresh thyme	1	bottle New Belgium Snap Shot

Place whole beets in a small roasting pan. A loaf pan would work great. Place sugar, thyme, salt, and beer into pan. Juice the orange into the pan and add the rind as well. Cover tightly with foil and place in 350° oven for about one hour. Pierce beets with a knife. The knife should go in and out smoothly. Once beets are cooked through, remove from the pan. Cool beets in refrigerator for about one hour. Once beets are cooled, carefully peel them and cut into large chunks.

CHEF'S NOTE: This could be done a day ahead to save time.

SNAPSHOT VINAIGRETTE

½	cup New Belgium Snap Shot (the rest is for drinking)	1	tablespoon fresh thyme
1	tablespoon orange zest	½	tablespoon celery salt
1	tablespoon shallot, chopped	¼	teaspoon black pepper
		2	cups canola oil

Place beer, orange zest, shallot, thyme, celery salt, and pepper in blender. Purée on high until smooth. Slowly drizzle in the oil until dressing emulsifies to a nice thick consistency.

CHEF'S NOTE: The vinaigrette recipe makes about six servings. It will keep in the refrigerator for about two weeks.

SALAD

1	head green leaf lettuce, chopped	½	cup toasted almond slivers
½	cup thinly sliced red onion	½	cup New Belgium Snap Shot Vinaigrette
1	cup goat cheese		

Toss the lettuce and onion with the vinaigrette. Top with almonds and goat cheese. Drink beer.

BREWER'S PAIRING: New Belgium Sunshine Wheat

The salad pairs perfectly with the Sunshine Wheat because they are both light, and slightly spicy with a tart finish. The orange peel and fruity notes from the coriander in the beer complement the citrus flavor and spiciness of the salad.

BREW MASTER'S SHIFT LAGER LOBSTER PO' BOY

COLLABORATION	NEW BELGIUM BREWING COMPANY Brewer, Grady Hull
	JAX FISH HOUSE Chef, Ricky Myers

PREP TIME: 30 minutes
4 SERVINGS

5	tablespoons butter
4	(6 inch) hoagie buns, pre-sliced
½	cup shallot, sliced
2	tablespoons garlic
½	pound sliced andouille sausage
1	cup fresh tomato, chopped
2	(4-6 ounce) fresh lobster tails, shelled and cut into ½ inch pieces
2	tablespoons chopped parsley
1	cup New Belgium Shift Lager
1	teaspoon salt
2	cups romaine lettuce, shredded
4	tablespoons spicy brown mustard

Spread about ½ tablespoon of butter on each bun and toast in a pan or in the oven until golden brown. Place two tablespoons of butter in medium sized sauté pan. Once butter is hot, add shallots, garlic and andouille to the pan. Once everything starts to brown, add tomato, lobster, and parsley. Once the tomatoes start to break down, add one cup of Shift Lager to the pan. Reduce the beer by about half. Add salt and the remaining butter to the pan and lightly stir with a wooden spoon until butter has melted.

TO SERVE: Spread the mustard evenly onto toasted buns. Evenly disperse lettuce and po' boy mix onto buns.

CHEF'S NOTE: Enjoy this po' boy for breakfast after a long night of drinking.

BREWER'S PAIRING: New Belgium Shift Lager
Light. Balanced. Drinkable. There is an approachable nature to both the sandwich and the beer—they don't overpower each other, and they both provide a nice balance. The key notes of the seafood flavor pair well with the tropical notes of the hops.

SEA BASS SNAPSHOT VERACRUZ

COLLABORATION	**NEW BELGIUM BREWING COMPANY** Brewer, Grady Hull
	JAWS SUSHI Chef, Jeff Nanbara

PREP TIME: 35 minutes
2-4 SERVINGS

2	tablespoons olive oil
½	red onion, diced
½	green pepper, diced
2	tomatoes, diced
2	tablespoons capers
1	jalapeño, sliced
20	green olives, sliced
2	cloves garlic
1	lime
2	striped sea bass, filleted
½	bottle of New Belgium Snapshot Wheat

In a large skillet, sauté olive oil, onions and garlic until onions are clear. Next add green peppers, tomatoes, capers, jalapeño, olives, a splash of Snapshot, and sauté for a couple of minutes. Clear out a portion of the skillet and place sea bass. Pour more Snapshot in, squeeze in some lime juice, and cook fish until starting to flake. You can flip the sea bass if needed or desired. Plate sea bass on a portion of rice (see Chef's Note) then scoop veggies and sauce over sea bass.

CHEF'S NOTE: As with any recipe, feel free to adjust any of these ingredients. If you like cilantro, then by all means chop some up and throw it in. For more heat add more jalapeños, or go with a different pepper. You can plate with any carbohydrate, so rice, mashed potatoes, noodles, or whatever works. Striped sea bass is available to me through our suppliers, but any light flaky white fish will do. The essence of the Veracruz style is the tomatoes, olives, capers and jalapeños so have fun!

BREWER'S PAIRING: New Belgium Slow Ride Session IPA
Slow Ride Session IPA complements the Veracruz as they are both light and have robust flavors. The beer has tropical citrus aromatics from the hops, which complement the savory notes from the olives, capers and bass.

UNAGI RAMPANT IPA NIGIRI SUSHI

COLLABORATION | **NEW BELGIUM BREWING COMPANY** Brewer, Grady Hull   **JAWS SUSHI** Chef, Jeff Nanbara

PREP TIME: 10 minutes if all prepared and cooked through
PREP TIME SUSHI RICE: 1½ hours
14 PIECES OF UNAGI SUSHI

	small batch of Sushi Rice		sesame seeds to taste
1	package of fresh water eel (Unagi)		teriyaki sauce to taste
1	package of nori sheets (seaweed sheet)	½	cup of New Belgium Rampant IPA
	wasabi to taste		
	pickled ginger to taste		

1 Cook and prepare the sushi rice. This is a task in itself that takes time and should not be taken lightly. It will be something that takes a bit of trial and error before achieving a desired result.

2 While you are waiting for the rice to cool, you can get the eel ready to be served. Open up the package of eel and slice eel to desired size (approximately 14 pieces in a package). When slicing, first cut the fillet in half lengthwise, then slice at a 45° angle, cutting each half into seven 1" x 4" pieces.

3 Place eel and the beer in a small oven safe dish. Heat to 180° or until bubbly.

4 Once the rice is cool enough to work with, form into small blocks and place an eel piece on top and secure with a strip of nori. Add on some teriyaki sauce and sprinkle with sesame seeds. Given the tropical notes to the Rampant beer from New Belgium, it is an excellent pairing with eel based sushi. Serve with side of wasabi and pickled ginger.

CHEF'S NOTE: Since sushi encompasses so many dishes you can be quite creative. You could also make a roll to be paired with Rampant that could include cream cheese, avocado, or even banana. The fresh water eel, nori, wasabi, and picked ginger can be found at an Asian specialty grocery store. If eel is frozen, then let it thaw out in the refrigerator until done and then cut into pieces. The sushi rice is medium grain Japanese rice that can be found at specialty stores or even your local grocery. Once the rice is cooked, mix in sushi vinegar, then let cool to just above room temperature. Now that you have the sushi rice you can make pieces or rolls and have fun!

BREWER'S PAIRING: New Belgium Snapshot Wheat
The beer and the sushi are light and both have some peppery notes. The Unagi pairs well with the herbal tones from the lactobacillus in the beer.

FCB

established 1992

Taylor Krantz **FCB**

Scott Olivo **FCB MODERN TAVERN**

Mike and Diane Del Duca **THE CHOCOLATE CAFÉ**

FCB COLLABORATIONS

TAYLOR KRANTZ, FCB

In 2010, Taylor and his brother-in-law Thomas, began exploring home brewing with a book and a small starter kit. "We initially started brewing three batches of beer and eventually made our own half-barrel system in the garage. Since we built it from the ground up, we learned a lot during those three years." Taylor's new infatuation for beer inspired him to apply his nutrition major towards brewing. He began an internship with FCB shortly after graduation, which quickly turned into a full time brewing career. "I love brewing because it's such an awesome mesh between science and artistry. You're able to do so much with it. You can envision it and then create it. That's what got me hooked." Taylor's talent for creating tasty brews is complemented by his amiable personality.

SCOTT OLIVO, FCB MODERN TAVERN

Scott's adventurous spirit and inclination for culinary curiosity led him on the trip of a lifetime. "I'm a recovering hippie. I used to hitchhike in my 20s on the west coast. It was hard, boring, and lonely—but the best times I've ever had," says Scott. He learned about organic vegan cooking by spending time in a Buddhist temple, built kitchens at rainbow gatherings, served food out of dirt ovens, and drummed with other transients on a beach. Near the end of his travels, he arrived in Telluride, Colorado, a small storybook town nestled in the heart of the San Juans, where he trained as a chef in a fine dining atmosphere. Currently serving as a chef at a restaurant inside of a brewery is an advantage for Scott as it enables him to work with his second love affair, beer. He has created an entire menu that offers a variety of handcrafted beer infused items. Scott pushes the boundaries of classic comfort food, like his dangerously delicious IPA Raspberry and Chocolate Stout Beer Doughnuts, or his juicy Tavern Burger grilled with smoky Chocolate Stout. In addition to his passion for cooking, he still strives to get in tune with his explorative nature. He spends as much time as he can in the outdoors with his wife Cindy and beloved dogs, Princess Leia, Luke Skywalker, and Maggie Magdalene.

MIKE & DIANE DEL DUCA, THE CHOCOLATE CAFÉ

Inspired by the cozy chocolate cafés dispersed throughout Europe, Mike Del Duca and his wife Diane decided to open their very own in Fort Collins. It was quite fitting because as Diane says, "Mike was born a chocoholic, and was convinced he didn't speak a whole year because he was thinking about chocolate." In 2007, they opened The Chocolate Café in Old Town with a vision to bring a homey and comfortable chocolate haven for the sweet tooths in the community. This came naturally for them because they are a very loving and welcoming couple. Most of their delightful desserts are homemade and will most definitely bring you back for more. To satisfy your savory side, they also offer a variety of lunch and dinner options like their creamy Three Cheese Mac and Cheese. Mike always has a new idea stirring for a delicious dessert or appetizer. Want a little taste of heaven? Stop by to try their Double Chocolate Bacon Stout Cheesecake. Stay tuned for more creative dishes!

PEACH BEERSALA WITH 1020 PALE ALE PORK LOIN MEDALLIONS

COLLABORATION | **FCB** Brewer, Taylor Krantz **FCB MODERN TAVERN** Chef, Scott Olivo

PREP TIME: 15-20 minutes
2 SERVINGS

3	(3 ounce) pork loin medallions, slightly pounded	½	teaspoon ground black pepper
	AP flour for dredge	½	teaspoon salt
3	tablespoons butter	¾	cup of FCB 1020 Pale Ale
3	tablespoons garlic, minced	¼	cup vegetable stock
4	tablespoons shallots, chopped	3	tablespoons grated parmesan
4	tablespoons shiitake mushrooms, sliced	4	tablespoons heavy cream
3	tablespoons + 1 tablespoon fresh peaches, peeled and diced	2	cups wild rice

1 Rinse pork medallions with water and pat dry, then dredge both sides in flour enough to slightly cover.

2 In large saucepan melt butter over medium heat. Add pork and cook for 1½ minutes per side. Remove to wire rack and set aside.

3 Immediately add garlic, mushrooms, shallots, and peaches to leftover butter. Sauté until tender, approximately three minutes.

4 Pour ¾ cups FCB 1020 Pale Ale directly into pan and the rest into a chilled glass to enjoy later.

5 Toss in salt and pepper and increase heat to medium high to reduce beer until liquid is almost gone, approximately four minutes.

6 Add vegetable stock and heavy cream, bring to a simmer.

7 Turn off heat and reintroduce pork to pan.

8 Serve with wild rice, parmesan cheese, and a sliced peach garnish.

LOCAL SOURCES

Pork from Cargill Meats, Fort Morgan, Co
Mushrooms from Hazel Dell, Fort Collins, Co
Peaches from Morton's Orchards, Palisade, Co

CHEF'S NOTE: Fresh peaches are always preferred, but in a pinch frozen peaches will work just fine for cooking.

BREWER'S PAIRING: FCB Red Banshee
The Peach Beersala with 1020 Pale Ale Pork Loin Medallions pairs perfectly with Red Banshee, highlighting the caramel and toffee profile of the brew. The earthiness of the mushrooms balances Red Banshee's malty sweetness.

BIG SHOT HAZELNUT BROWN ALE PECAN PIE

COLLABORATION | **FCB** Brewer, Taylor Krantz **FCB MODERN TAVERN** Chef, Scott Olivo

PREP TIME: 35 minutes
6-8 SERVINGS

1	pre-made piecrust		⅓	cup + ¼ cup FCB Big Shot Hazelnut Brown Ale
5	tablespoons + 2 tablespoons butter		2	cups pecans
⅓	cup brown sugar		1	teaspoon vanilla
¾	cup corn syrup		3	eggs, lightly beaten
½	teaspoon salt		1	granny smith apple, sliced and poached

Roll out pie dough and shape to 8" pie pan. Poke holes in bottom. Place in freezer for 20-25 minutes or until very firm. Line pie shell with parchment paper and fill with rice or pie weights. Bake at 350° for 10 minutes. Remove rice or weights and bake for another five minutes.

In a saucepan, combine butter, brown sugar, corn syrup, salt, and melt together until smooth. Remove from heat and whisk in eggs until smooth. Add Big Shot Hazelnut Brown Ale, vanilla and 1½ cups pecans. Pour into the pie shell and top with remaining ½ cup whole pecans in a pattern. Continue baking at 350° for 30 minutes, rotating halfway through. Remove and cool when pie is set. Serve at room temperature or warm.

While pie is baking, poach sliced apple in two tablespoons butter and ¼ cup Big Shot for five minutes or until soft. Remove and cool. Garnish with poached apple slices. When pie is set, serve at room temperature or warm.

CHEF'S NOTE: While slicing your fruit, a few drops of lime juice in water will help keep your slices from turning brown.

BREWER'S PAIRING: FCB Chocolate Stout
In the pecan pie, the apples help lighten the dish by bringing a nice tartness to pair with the sweet and roast flavors.

"MIKE WAS BORN A CHOCOHOLIC, AND WAS CONVINCED HE DIDN'T SPEAK A WHOLE YEAR BECAUSE HE WAS THINKING ABOUT CHOCOLATE."

- DIANE DEL DUCA

BACON STOUT CHOCOLATE CHEESECAKE

COLLABORATION | **FCB** Brewer, Taylor Krantz
| **THE CHOCOLATE CAFÉ** Chefs, Mike & Diane Del Duca

PREP TIME: 45 minutes
PAN PREP: 1 (10 inch) spring form pan-parchment paper, or non-stick pan spray
10 SERVINGS

CRUST:

½	cup graham cracker crumbs
1	cup pretzel crumbs
2	tablespoons sugar
6	tablespoons butter, melted

FILLING:

8	ounces FCB Chocolate Stout
7	ounces dark chocolate

3	(8 ounce package) cream cheese (room temperature)
1¼	cup sugar
3	eggs
2	tablespoons flour
⅓	cup cocoa powder
1	tablespoon espresso powder

CRUST:

Pat all mixed ingredients into bottom of pan. Do not prebake crust.

FILLING:

1. Take the Chocolate Stout and chocolate and melt them over medium heat. Set aside to cool to create a chocolate mixture.
2. While that is cooling, combine the cream cheese and sugar in mixer bowl and cream until smooth.
3. Add eggs one at a time, scraping the bottom of the mixer bowl after each egg.
4. Pour the cooled chocolate beer mixture into cream cheese and mix well, scraping bowl.
5. Add flour, cocoa powder and espresso powder. Stir until just combined. Scrape bowl.
6. Pour onto crust and bake for 45-50 minutes in 350° oven.

BEER CANDIED BACON

PAN PREP: Baking sheets lined with parchment paper

16	slices bacon		⅓	cup FCB Chocolate Stout
½	cup brown sugar			

Mix brown sugar and beer. Using pastry brush, brush liquid on bacon. Bake 10 minutes in 350° oven. Remove from oven, flip bacon and coat with liquid. Bake 10 minutes. If there is leftover liquid, coat bacon again and bake until darkened… not burned. Cool and chop into small pieces. Refrigerate.

CHEF'S NOTE: Spray your baking pan before you candy your bacon. It's tough to clean if you don't. Make sure the bacon is very crisp and candied. In other words you want the sugar to be brittle. You don't want soggy bacon!

BREWER'S PAIRING: FCB Chocolate Stout
The chocolate and roast flavors from the Chocolate Stout helps temper some of the sweetness in the two desserts. The salty bacon helps accentuate the roast character and exemplify the bold flavors in the cheesecake.

C.B. & POTTS RESTAURANT & BREWERY

established 1996

Joe Bowden C.B. & POTTS RESTAURANT & BREWERY

Nick Anderson C.B. & POTTS RESTAURANT & BREWERY

Tony Tyler CAFÉ ATHENS

C.B. & POTTS RESTAURANT & BREWERY COLLABORATIONS

C.B. & POTTS RESTAURANT & BREWERY
and CAFÉ ATHENS

JOE BOWDEN, C.B. & POTTS RESTAURANT & BREWERY

Meet Joe—The punk rocker scientist turned brewer. There's no doubt about it, Joe is one loveable brewer! He is known for making quality beer and being loyal to the beer community. His journey getting there is a good one. Joe started in college in a small rural southern town where craft beer wasn't prevalent. He would drive an hour to seek out new and exciting beers and later decided to build his own brewing equipment. Before he knew it, he was brewing beers for local parties. His passion for beer only grew stronger when he moved to Fort Collins for graduate school in Horticulture. "Colorado changed everything because I was so inspired by great breweries and good beer." While he was in school, he continued brewing during his spare time, became president of the home brewer club, and eventually started working at Equinox Brewing Company. When an opportunity to seize a career as a head brewer arose at C.B. & Potts, Joe eagerly pursued it. Although he left the horticulture path, his inner science nerd self is still thriving. "With my geeky science background, I don't think there's anybody out there that geeks out more on beer than myself." What Joe loves most about brewing is focusing on two different aspects of pub brewing—the scientific/technical components of brewing flagship beers, and the creative element of creating ever-changing seasonal beers. When Joe is not in his "beer lab," he is found fly fishing, baking bread, spending time with his family, and playing or listening to music. It wouldn't be unusual to find Joe listening to 90s punk music while cleaning beer tanks.

NICK ANDERSON, C.B. & POTTS RESTAURANT & BREWERY

Nick Anderson has a great heart for people—whether it's in the kitchen with his co-workers or on the football field with his team. This is evident by the way he genuinely cares for and interacts with others. He is recognized as being empathetic to his co-workers and often lends an ear to anyone in need. "I love helping people and making a difference in their lives. In high school, I was always the captain of my sports teams and found that I could make a difference through leadership roles." Nick fell into cooking when he started working at C.B. & Potts while studying to be a social worker at CSU. He has discovered that "career paths aren't defined by what you've learned in school, it's by a passion that needs to be followed." After completing his degree, he realized that his interest for cooking exceeded his interest to be a social worker. "My desire for helping people was redirected to food which was a void that needed to be filled in my life." Nick loves to prepare meals and watch his customers become happier through his creations. He has found that spending time with his friends and family is important to him. His recent favorite activity is grabbing a great beer while playing pool.

TONY TYLER, CAFÉ ATHENS

Tony is a happy-go-lucky fitness and culinary enthusiast. "I love living a healthy lifestyle, but I also love eating food too! I'm a fat kid at heart." While studying health and exercise science at CSU, Tony began cooking at Renzio's Grill and built great working relationships with the owners, Cary and Dell Deschene. "They became father figures to me—I was part of the family." Impressed by Tony's hard work and dedication, they asked him to work as a chef at their new restaurant, Café Athens. Tony accepted and was given the opportunity to apply his degree towards designing a nutritious menu. "I wanted to help Café Athens become more successful so I tried to come up with healthy creations. Instead of offering standard dishes such as the gyro, I created a nourishing chicken kabob." Tony continues dish development at a variety of levels. He particularly enjoys discovering the new flavors that arise once beer is added to his dishes, such as his Lamb Porter Stout Kabob. "Adding beer to lamb enhanced its flavor and juiciness, and I noticed it wasn't as tough. Being able to cook with beer opened my eyes to how I could mix it in and what it does with certain foods. It made a whole world of difference." His love for food is balanced by spending time with his family and friends, and cheering on Colorado athletics.

BBQ PORK RIBS

COLLABORATION	C.B. & POTTS RESTAURANT & BREWERY Brewer, Joe Bowden
	C.B. & POTTS RESTAURANT & BREWERY Chef, Nick Anderson

PREP TIME: 4½ hours
4 HALF RACKS

2	racks pork baby back ribs		**SECOND BBQ SAUCE (BASTING)**
1	ounce premixed seasoning blend (your favorite)	4	ounces Sweet Baby Rays BBQ
2	cups Sweet Baby Rays BBQ		**BRAISING LIQUID**
		2	cups water
	FIRST BBQ SAUCE	1	cup C.B. & Potts Big Red IPA
⅔	Sweet Baby Rays BBQ	1	cup beef broth
⅓	Molasses		

Cut both racks of ribs in half. Rub seasoning blend onto each rack of ribs. Place ribs into a baking dish (a casserole dish or roasting pan will both work well) and add the braising liquid ingredients. Cover with plastic wrap, and then aluminum foil. Cook in preheated oven at 275° for 3½ hours. Time may need adjusting based on your oven.

Pull ribs out of the oven, drain liquid and allow to cool slightly. Coat ribs with the First BBQ sauce (combine mix). The ribs can then be plastic wrapped and held for grilling later. If you intend to grill the ribs more than two days later, you should freeze them and pull them the day before you grill.

Preheat the grill, and then place the ribs on the hot grill meat side down. Baste the backside of each rack with ½ ounce of Second BBQ Sauce (Basting). Cook for about two minutes. Turn the ribs 90° to create diamond marks, cooking for another two minutes. Turn the ribs over, baste with another ½ ounce of Second BBQ Sauce (Baste) and cook for about three minutes to an internal temperature of 165°.

Pull the ribs off the grill and serve with your favorite side.

CHEF'S NOTE: For the ribs, make sure the meat falls off the bone when you take it off the grill. Pairs well with any heavy starch, we use BBQ baked beans, French fries and coleslaw.

BREWER'S PAIRING: C.B. & Potts Total Disorder Porter
I love to pair porters with grilled foods. The medium body of brown porters along with the chocolate, coffee, and light toffee notes are a perfect complement to charred and smoky grill flavors.

BIG HORN HEFEWEIZEN MAHI MAHI FISH TACOS

COLLABORATION | **C.B. & POTTS RESTAURANT & BREWERY** Brewer, Joe Bowden
C.B. & POTTS RESTAURANT & BREWERY Chef, Nick Anderson

PREP TIME: 30 minutes
4 SERVINGS

1	pound Mahi Mahi, cut into 2 ounce filets
2	ounces all-purpose flour

TEMPURA BATTER

5	ounces tempura flour
6	ounces C.B. & Potts Big Horn Hefeweizen Beer
2½	ounces club soda
1	teaspoon salt
1	teaspoon pepper
1	teaspoon garlic blend

SPICY RANCH COLESLAW

8	ounces shredded green cabbage
2	ounces spicy ranch
1	ounce pickled red onions
4	tablespoons green onions, sliced at an angle

GARNISHES

8	ounces pico de gallo (use your favorite recipe or buy at the store)
8	lime wedges

Serve with 8 (6 inch) flour or corn tortillas

1 Make the tempura batter by mixing tempura flour, Big Horn Hefeweizen, club soda, and seasoning. Use a whisk and mix until smooth with no lumps.

2 Make spicy coleslaw by mixing shredded cabbage with the green onions, pickled red onions (you can pickle red onions by soaking them in rice wine vinegar with sugar and salt dissolved in it), and spicy ranch (or better yet a chipotle tarragon dressing if you can find one).

3 Set deep fryer to 325°. If you do not have a deep fryer you can also pan fry, sear, or blacken the Mahi (most fish cooked medium should take about five minutes).

4 Coat the Mahi Mahi in all-purpose flour. Then dip into the tempura batter, cover completely, but allow some of the excess to drip off.

5 You will need to batter and fry the fish in small batches depending on how much frying space you have.

6 Fry the fish to an internal temperature of 145°, should be about five minutes.

7 Place fried fish onto a plate lined with paper towels to soak up some of the excess oil.

9 Warm up the tortillas by gently microwaving (30-45 seconds should work well).

10 Spread the coleslaw mix out evenly between all of the tortillas.

11 Place one piece of fried Mahi Mahi on top of the coleslaw mix.

12 Place one ounce of pico de gallo on top of each piece of Mahi Mahi, then garnish with a piece of lime.

13 Serve the tacos.

CHEF'S NOTE: When you're making your batter, be sure to use fresh club soda and beer so the batter doesn't go bad on you. The food will taste flat if you don't. Make sure club soda and beer are well carbonated to make batter light and fluffy. I suggest you serve it with black beans, Spanish rice, and salsa.

BREWER'S PAIRING: C.B. & Potts Big Horn Hefeweizen
When I'm cooking with beer, I often prefer to pair the meal with a different beer than the one I was cooking with. However, in this case, I really enjoy the way the creamy and highly effervescent hefeweizen can cut through a fried tempura batter.

TOTAL DISORDER PORTER HOT FUDGE BROWNIE SUNDAE

COLLABORATION | **C.B. & POTTS RESTAURANT & BREWERY** Brewer, Joe Bowden
C.B. & POTTS RESTAURANT & BREWERY Chef, Nick Anderson

PREP TIME: 30 minutes
4 SERVINGS

4   (6") circle shaped brownies (Krusteaz makes a great pre-made mix that requires only water and cooks well at altitude)

1   pound vanilla ice cream

9   ounces hot fudge

6   ounces C.B. & Potts Total Disorder Porter

4   ounces whipped cream

⅓   ounce brown sugar

4   ounces Hershey's chocolate syrup

1   ounce almonds, sliced and toasted

1 Bake the brownies according to the box or your favorite recipe.

2 Make the porter fudge. Combine the Total Disorder Porter with the brown sugar in a small sauté pan.

3 Boil the beer and sugar mix on medium high heat until it has reduced in volume by half. Pull off of the heat. Allow to cool slightly.

4 Mix the cooked beer with warmed hot fudge. You now have Total Disorder Porter Hot Fudge.

5 Assemble the dessert. Squeeze one ounce of Hershey's chocolate syrup into the bottom of four bowls.

6 Warm up the brownie circle gently in the microwave (about 45 seconds each should do) and place onto the pool of chocolate syrup.

7 Top each brownie with four ounces of vanilla ice cream.

8 Top the ice cream with three ounces of warmed Total Disorder Porter Hot Fudge.

9 Add whipped cream to the top and finish with toasted almond slices.

CHEF'S NOTE: Make sure to use high altitude mix. Scoop with your favorite kind of ice cream..

BREWER'S PAIRING: C.B. & Potts 71 Pale Ale
Remember that sweet desserts will only amplify the naturally sweet characters from malted grains. Pale ales like our 71 Pale Ale have a nice balanced hoppy to malty profile and keep your sweet tooth in check.

ZEUS' CHILI NACHO DIP

COLLABORATION	**C.B. & POTTS RESTAURANT & BREWERY** Brewer, Joe Bowden **CAFÉ ATHENS** Chef, Tony Tyler

PREP TIME: 3 hours
25 SERVINGS

5	cups C.B. & Potts Total Disorder Porter
4	cups beef chili sauce
½	cup salsa
¼	cup diced green onions
1	cup diced tomatoes
1	cup green chiles
½	cup pinto beans
1	block of Velveeta cheese
3/4	cup of Kasseri cheese

In a crockpot, pour in C.B. & Potts Total Disorder Porter. Add in beef chili sauce, salsa, diced green onions, diced tomatoes, green chiles, and ½ cup of pinto beans. Then, get a block of Velveeta cheese and cut off six ½ inch slices and layer them on top.

Top it off with Kasseri cheese and keep the crockpot on low heat for about 2½ hours. Mix it and let it sit for another 30 minutes and it will be ready to serve.

CHEF'S NOTE: You can add more Kasseri cheese to strengthen the taste.

BREWER'S PAIRING: C.B. & Potts Buttface Amber Ale
C.B. & Potts Buttface Amber Ale and nachos go well together. This Greek twist is no exception.

TZATZIKI BLONDE SAUCE

COLLABORATION | **C.B. & POTTS RESTAURANT & BREWERY**
Brewer, Joe Bowden
CAFÉ ATHENS Chef, Tony Tyler

PREP TIME: 7 minutes
10-15 SERVINGS

½	liter of plain yogurt
½	cucumber
4	tablespoons of Greek spices
3	teaspoons C.B. & Potts Colorado Blonde
1	teaspoon soy oil

You want to start off with plain yogurt in a container. Next, use a vegetable peeler and peel cucumber into the container. Make sure the slices are very thin all the way around. Then add Greek spices, C.B. & Potts Colorado Blonde, and soy oil. Mix it very well with a spoon or in a blender to a creamy state and refrigerate if you are serving later.

🖊 **CHEF'S NOTE:** If it tastes too strong, add more yogurt. To strengthen the flavor, add more beer.

🍺 **BREWER'S PAIRING:** C.B. & Potts Colorado Blonde
Just like when you're cooking delicate sauces with beer, when pairing beers with lighter fair try not to overwhelm the palate. A crisp and easy drinking beer like our Colorado Blonde is often an excellent choice.

LAMB OR STEAK MARINADE

COLLABORATION	**C.B. & POTTS RESTAURANT & BREWERY** Brewer, Joe Bowden **CAFÉ ATHENS** Chef, Tony Tyler

PREP TIME: 5 minutes
8-10 SERVINGS

½	liter C.B. & Potts Total Disorder Porter
½	liter soy oil
2	teaspoons lemon juice
1	teaspoon garlic powder
1	teaspoon black pepper
1	teaspoon cayenne pepper
	pinch of salt

In a container, combine C.B. & Potts Total Disorder Porter with soy oil. Add in lemon juice, garlic powder, black pepper, and cayenne pepper. Finish it off with a pinch of salt. Stir it together.

CHEF'S NOTE: When serving, you should soak the meat in the marinade for about 10 minutes to make the meat more tender and juicy.

BREWER'S PAIRING: C.B. & Potts Big Red IPA
Marinades are a great way to infuse beer flavors into foods. Don't forget to consider contact time, temperature, and the type of food you're marinating. I would avoid using overly hoppy beers since the bitterness can be concentrated when cooked. Stronger foods can take marinades made with stronger flavored beers, and also pair well with stronger beers like Big Red IPA.

> "I LOVE LIVING A HEALTHY LIFESTYLE, BUT I ALSO LOVE EATING FOOD TOO! I'M A FAT KID AT HEART."
>
> - TONY TYLER

FUNKWERKS BREWERY

established 2009

Gordon Schuck FUNKWERKS BREWERY

Amelia Mouton RESTAURANT 415

Dana DeMarco CAFÉ VINO

FUNKWERKS BREWERY COLLABORATIONS

GORDON SCHUCK, FUNKWERKS BREWERY

Gordon is the "Splinter" of the Ninja Turtles to the brewers in the community. Several brewers look up to him as he often acts as their mentor. "When I first started, I received a lot of help from other breweries in town like New Belgium and Odell. Helping some of the newer breweries gave me an opportunity to pass on the knowledge." Before brewing, Gordon was in school for electrical engineering and pursued a career building bike frames out of his garage to complement his love for mountain biking. Shortly after, he became interested in home brewing as a fun side hobby. "After I was given a brewing kit, next thing I knew a passion for brewing came over me. I wanted to find out everything I needed to know about beer. I'm the kind of person that follows my passion. When I'm into mountain biking and racing, I'm consumed by it. The same thing happened when I started brewing. I heard my calling and went for it." This desire to brew led Gordon to Seibel Institute in Chicago, Illinois, where he met his friend and future business partner, Brad Lincoln. With Gordon's strong desire to brew and Brad's savvy business skills, a perfect team was formed. In 2009, they launched Funkwerks, initially focusing on the saison style, and later branching out to other Belgian styles. When walking into their colorful taproom, life gets a little happier being in the presence of several of Gordon's award winning beers (four GABF awards, one World Beer Cup, and Small Brewery of the year 2012). Outside of the brewery, Gordon likes to cook and collaborate with chefs as well spending time with his beautiful wife Carolee, and his dog Ana.

AMELIA MOUTON, RESTAURANT 415

If you have recently tuned into The Food Network, you may have noticed chef Amelia, featured in Diners, Drive-Ins and Dives, showcasing her savory cauliflower steak and tasty chickpea pizza. Amelia is a Fort Collins native with a mission to bring joy to the table. "I always loved how food brought joy to my family when we would all get together, and wanted to learn how to cook so I could continue bringing happiness to others." She credits her crash course in culinary arts to her work on a fly fishing ranch in Ohio where she prepared lunches for boat guides and was given flexibility to make whatever she wanted. From there, she returned home to Colorado, and began baking and catering elegant wedding cakes for a Fort Collins favorite, and her father's restaurant, The Rio Grande. The two dollar taco shop she and her father launched gave her a glimpse of running a restaurant, which led to the opening of Restaurant 415 with her father and two other business partners. She was gladly given free range of the menu. "I wanted to create something that people would feel light and healthy after they ate. They could indulge a little, but could also come here on a date and could make out afterward," laughs Amelia. Her playful personality, warmth, and boundless curiosity for cuisine are reflected in her dishes. Beyond the kitchen, Amelia enjoys laughing, dancing, and traveling.

DANA DEMARCO, CAFÉ VINO

With both Italian and Greek roots, Dana was given the gift of international culinary appreciation from an early age. "I often visited my father's side of the family in Italy where we cooked as a family. We went in September, when the tomatoes were in season and incorporated them into almost every meal." Dana's interest for cooking developed when she was 16 years old. "Initially, I wanted to work in the medical field. However, in High School I often found myself running out of the lab and throwing up after dissecting frogs so I turned to the culinary arts instead." Dana became eager to learn more about culinary arts when her friend attended culinary school at Johnson and Wales. She often asked questions about what her friend learned in her classes and became further interested in learning to cook. An opportunity to gain experience as a chef presented itself after meeting her new mentor Somi, an owner of a local restaurant. Somi taught Dana the fundamentals of cooking and gave her a scholarship to begin an apprenticeship at Fort Collins Country Club. Since then, Dana has flourished as a cook and worked with several respected chefs in Fort Collins at staple restaurants including Jax Fish House, Canyon Chop House, The Kitchen, and Café Vino. Her latest interests are reading on foraging, as well as studying the planets and stars.

ROASTED JALAPEÑO DECEIT MAC AND CHEESE

COLLABORATION | **FUNKWERKS** Brewer, Gordon Schuck   **RESTAURANT 415** Chef, Amelia Mouton

PREP TIME: 30 minutes
BAKE TIME: 30 minutes
8-10 SERVINGS

3	jalapeños	9	cups Cozy Cow Funkwerks Tropic King cheddar, grated (reserve 1 cup on the side to top the mac)
1½	pounds macaroni noodles or cavatappi noodles (for gluten free, sub brown rice noodles)	4	cups Cozy Cow jalapeño cheddar cheese, grated
7	cups milk (we use Morning Fresh at the 415)	1	cup unsalted butter
4	cups heavy cream	1	cup flour (for gluten free, sub brown rice flour)
1	tablespoon salt	1	cup Funkwerks Deceit
1	teaspoon pepper	1	tablespoon dijon mustard
1	teaspoon cayenne	2	cups breadcrumbs

Roast your jalapeños in a 400° oven until the outside is charred, peel skin and dice. You can keep the seeds if you like it super spicy, or deseed if spice isn't nice to you. Omit jalapeños all together if you prefer! In a medium to large pot on medium high heat melt the butter. Add flour and whisk creating a roux. Add your milk and cream, whisking until it starts to thicken. In seven to10 minutes it should coat a spoon.

Once thickened, turn off heat and add your mustard, spices and cheese until it is melted and mixed together. Whisk in Deceit beer (it may start to curdle a little from the alcohol but once you bake it, it will become creamy again). Bring a pot of water to boil, add your pasta and cook al dente (five to seven minutes). It's best to undercook than overcook; it will fully cook when baked.

Drain your pasta and mix into sauce. Add jalapeños as well. In a 9" x 15" oven safe pan, place your sauce and noodles. Top with remaining cheese, sprinkle with breadcrumbs, and bake in a 400° oven until top is browned a bit (15 minutes). Crack open a bottle of Deceit and enjoy!

CHEF'S NOTE: You can omit jalapeños and add other veggies like steamed broccoli or cauliflower. You can add bacon in the mix—get creative! Be sure to taste everything along the way to make sure you like the flavors and adjust accordingly. Before baking, sauce might be kind of watered down, but will thicken back up once it's in the oven again. Throw a fried egg over top to eat for breakfast!

BREWER'S PAIRING: Funkwerks Deceit
Deceit has a nice spicy note from the combination of the yeast strain and the Saaz hops. This pairs wonderfully and complements the spices in the recipe and adds depth to the cheese.

ORANGE CREAM TROPIC KING CUPCAKES

COLLABORATION | **FUNKWERKS BREWERY** Brewer, Gordon Schuck   **RESTAURANT 415** Chef, Amelia Mouton

PREP TIME: 1 hour
24 SERVINGS

2	cups flour	1½	teaspoon orange zest, finely grated
¼	teaspoon baking powder	2	eggs
¼	teaspoon baking soda	½	cup Funkwerks Tropic King
¼	teaspoon salt	½	cup milk, room temperature
½	cup butter, room temperature	¼	cup orange juice
1	cup sugar	2	teaspoons vanilla

Preheat oven to 300°. Using a stand or hand mixer, cream together butter and sugar. In a separate bowl, whisk together the flour, baking powder, baking soda and salt, and then set aside. Add vanilla to butter/sugar mixture, add eggs one at a time, mixing well. Add orange zest, and then alternate between adding flour mixture and milk until it's all mixed together. Add Tropic King and orange juice. Batter might be slightly curdled and more wet than other cupcake recipes, but it's ok, it will all bake well. Bake in the oven for 10-20 minutes until tops are a golden brown and a toothpick comes out clean. Cool cupcakes and frost.

ORANGE CREAM FROSTING

1	cup unsalted butter, softened	1	tablespoon vanilla
8	ounces cream cheese, softened	1	cup orange juice
6	cups powdered sugar	1	cup Funkwerks Tropic King
½	teaspoon salt		

In a small saucepan boil the orange juice and Tropic King together. Let it simmer until it reduces into an almost honey-like texture (could take up to 30 minutes). Using a hand mixer or stand mixer, whip the butter and cream cheese together, then add the powdered sugar and salt. Add vanilla and two tablespoons of your cooled beer/orange juice reduction. Whip one last time. Frost your cooled cupcakes; you can decorate with some fresh orange zest.

CHEF'S NOTE: To decorate, use orange sprinkles or orange zest. You can also make candied orange zest to be super duper fancy! Throw chocolate chips in the batter if you want that chocolate covered orange flavor. Try not to open oven door during cooking process. This will help the cupcakes rise and stay risen. If you must peek at them, close oven door slowly with low force. If the frosting is too sweet for you, add ½ teaspoon of salt.

BREWER'S PAIRING: Funkwerks Tropic King
Tropic King has a unique hop that has a wonderful tropical fruit quality to it that blends well with the orange of the cupcakes. The high carbonation of the beer also helps cut through the cream cheese frosting and cleanse the palate for the next bite.

"SINCE I LOVE COOKING MYSELF, IT WAS A REAL LEARNING EXPERIENCE FOR ME TO SEE HOW AMELIA AND DANA USED FLAVORS TO CREATE THESE NEW DISHES. I WANT TO COLLABORATE AGAIN WITH AMELIA SO SHE CAN BRING MORE CUPCAKES. I DID IT FOR THE CUPCAKES."

-GORDON SCHUCK

"WE HAVE SOME PRETTY AMAZING BREWERIES IN TOWN THAT PRODUCE GREAT BEERS. I'M HAPPY I WAS PAIRED WITH GORDON FOR THIS BOOK BECAUSE HE IS SO MUCH FUN AND HELPS OPERATE A GREAT BREWERY."

- DANA DEMARCO

DECEIT PASTA WITH BALSALMIC TROPIC KING MACERATED TOMATOES

COLLABORATION | **FUNKWERKS BREWERY** Brewer, Gordon Schuck **CAFÉ VINO** Chef, Dana DeMarco

DECEIT PASTA DOUGH

PREP TIME: approximately 2 hours
YIELDS 1/2 POUND

3	eggs, room temperature	3 ½	cups all purpose flour
1	tablespoon extra virgin olive oil	2	cups Funkwerks Deceit
½	teaspoon kosher salt		

In a saucepan, reduce beer to ½ cup and let cool. In a mixer with the dough hook, add the flour. In a separate bowl, whisk together the eggs, oil, salt, and beer reduction. With the mixer on medium-low speed, use the dough hook to slowly incorporate the egg mixture into the flour. Allow the dough to mix for approximately 10 minutes. The dough should not be wet or sticky. Small pinches of flour may need to be kneaded into the dough until it is smooth and somewhat stiff. Divide the dough in half, wrap in plastic wrap, and let sit at room temperature for one hour before forming into desired shape.

BALSAMIC TROPIC KING MACERATED TOMATOES

PREP TIME: 1 hour
YIELDS 2 CUPS

2	cups Funkwerks Tropic King	¼	cup extra virgin olive oil
½	cup balsamic vinegar	½	teaspoon kosher salt
½	teaspoon red pepper flakes	¼	teaspoon black pepper
1½	pounds roma tomatoes, quartered		

Combine all ingredients in a medium saucepan. Simmer over medium-high heat for approximately 45 minutes or until tomatoes are soft and sauce is slightly syrupy.

CHEF'S NOTE: The pasta and the tomatoes are lovely with Merguez sausage, spinach and green beans sautéed together. Swirl in a little butter at the end.

BREWER'S PAIRING: Funkwerks Tropic King
Our house Saison yeast strain that we use in Tropic King has notes of pepper and ginger that adds complexity to the macerated tomatoes. The Deceit addition to the dough makes for a delicious and tender pasta. The combination is fantastic.

FUNKWERKS DECEIT CARAMEL & GRILLED PALISADE PEACHES

COLLABORATION | **FUNKWERKS BREWERY** Brewer, Gordon Schuck **CAFÉ VINO** Chef, Dana DeMarco

FUNKWERKS DECEIT CARAMEL

PREP TIME: approximately 30 minutes
YIELDS 8 OUNCES

½	cup heavy cream	1	cup granulated sugar
¼	cup Funkwerks Deceit	¼	teaspoon kosher salt

Put two tablespoons of sugar in a heavy bottomed, non-reactive saucepan over medium-high heat. Once sugar starts to turn amber colored in places, start to stir gently, and add another two tablespoons of sugar in the pan. Add remainder of the sugar to the saucepan in two tablespoon increments, allowing most of the sugar to melt before adding more. Once caramel has turned into a dark amber color, remove from heat and immediately add the cream and beer. Use caution, the mixture will steam and bubble! Stir until the cream and beer are completely incorporated. Stir in salt and allow to cool at room temperature. Refrigerate once cooled.

CHEF'S NOTE: Do not walk away from this sauce; sugar can burn in the blink of an eye.

GRILLED PALISADE PEACH

PREP TIME: 1 hour and 15 minutes – overnight
4 SERVINGS

2	Palisade Peaches, halved and pitted	1	teaspoon ground cinnamon
1	tablespoon brown sugar	½	teaspoon ground ginger
1	tablespoon granulated sugar	¼	teaspoon ground cloves
¼	teaspoon kosher salt		pan spray

Place peaches flesh side up on a plate. Combine remaining ingredients in a small mixing bowl until evenly distributed. Sprinkle on top of peaches; let cure for a minimum of one hour or overnight. Spray peaches with pan spray. Turn grill on high and make sure it's really hot before placing peaches sugared side down on it. Do not flip them over during grilling. Cook until there are grill marks on the bottom of the peach and the top feels soft to the touch.

CHEF'S NOTE: Serve with vanilla ice cream, Deceit caramel, and toasted almonds.

BREWER'S PAIRING: Funkwerks Deceit
Deceit is fermented quite warm resulting in the fruity aroma. Mixed with the caramel, it complements the peaches nicely.

EQUINOX BREWING

established 2010

Jared Lydon **EQUINOX BREWING**

Tim Downey **THE MELTING POT**

Jean Claude **LA CREPERIE & FRENCH BAKERY OF FORT COLLINS**

EQUINOX COLLABORATIONS

THE MELTING POT *and*
LA CREPERIE AND FRENCH BAKERY OF FORT COLLINS

JARED LYDON, EQUINOX BREWERY

Jared's heart beats to the sound of music and beer. Originally from New England, he moved to Fort Collins in 2007 for the music scene, and to study business at CSU. Jared biked to Equinox Brewing intermittently between his classes where he began to feel at home. Most of his class projects revolved around the brewery industry because of his developing fascination for beer. His hard work and loveable personality eventually landed him his dream job at Equinox Brewing. Colin Wescott, owner of Equinox explains, "Jared didn't have experience, but he had passion and heart and I wanted to take him on as an employee." While Jared served beer for three months in the taproom, Colin noticed his interest and potential for brewing and gave him the chance of a lifetime. Jared has a great respect and appreciation for Colin and the opportunity he gave him. "Colin has 20 years of professional brewing experience and took me under his wing. He was my Mr. Miagi and taught me everything I know about brewing." Jared continues, "I love everything about this place and being a brewer. My job is to make the best beer I can and to show how much I care about everybody through brewing." Jared also gives a lot of attention to his furry friends at home—his cat Walfreda, and dogs Tatanka and P.Y.T (Pretty Young Thing). His greatest joy is spending time with his new baby, Izabel.

TIM DOWNEY, THE MELTING POT

Tim Downey is dedicated to putting the fun in fondue while managing The Melting Pot in Fort Collins. He often passes on ancient fondue traditions to his guests such as, "If a man drops a piece of bread in the fondue, he has to buy the next bottle of wine. If a lady drops it, she has to kiss the guy on the right or host the next fondue party." Fondue is unique in that the guest is the true chef because they prepare the fondue themselves. As customers sip on a glass of wine and dip their skewers into the delicious steamy melted cheese and chocolate, Tim ensures an exquisite customer experience. He is determined to provide the perfect night out to his guests and acts as a catalyst in creating the optimal dining event. "I believe in strong relationships and bringing personality to all of our guests. The greatest part of my job is that it is guest driven, and I work on helping customers create memories and nice conversations." Tim continually gathers ideas with his staff to help best serve his guests. He is not only a fondue lover, but also a devoted family man. His favorite activities are fishing, golfing, and playing backyard soccer with his wife and children.

CLAUDE, LA CREPERIE AND FRENCH BAKERY OF FORT COLLINS

"I fell in love with baking and was literally hooked when I was three years old and accidently got stuck in the mixer. Since then, I haven't been able to stop," laughs Claude. Born and raised in Britany, France, Claude grew up with baking. As a child, his playground was his father's 45-year-old bakery. He remembers sneaking into his kitchen and baking fresh homemade croissants or baguettes at night when he couldn't sleep. Claude spent summers at his Grandma's farm where she made crepes all day and taught him the family's secret crepe recipe. His desire to continue baking stayed with him throughout his teenage years as he worked alongside his father. His father's happy spirit and dedication to baking influenced Claude to continue the family tradition. In his 20s he decided to move to Paris to gain more professional baking training. Aside from working at a bakery, he took baking classes and was trained by some of the top French bakers in Paris. Claude later decided to bring a taste of France to America, and opened Le Creperie, focusing on delicious hand crafted crepes. "If you have been to France and devoured their delicious crepes, you will find the same product at my Creperie." Claude showcases both sweet and savory options. For example, he offers the traditional Buckwheat Flour Gallete, which is extremely rare to find in the states. When Claude has a moment to relax, you may find him holding a glass of red wine and a paintbrush. Most of the impressive traditional French paintings seen on the walls at his restaurant are his very own masterpieces.

"I LOVE EVERYTHING ABOUT THIS PLACE AND BEING A BREWER. MY JOB IS TO MAKE THE BEST BEER I CAN AND TO SHOW HOW MUCH I CARE ABOUT EVERYBODY THROUGH BREWING."

- JARED LYON

NIGHT RYDER MUNICH DUNKEL CHEDDAR FONDUE

| COLLABORATION | EQUINOX BREWING Brewer, Jared Lyon |
| | THE MELTING POT Chef, Tim Downey |

PREP TIME: 10 minutes
4-6 SERVINGS

2¾	cups shredded cheddar cheese
3	tablespoons all purpose flour
1	cup Equinox Night Ryder Munich Dunkel beer
2	teaspoons garlic, chopped
2	teaspoons shallots, chopped
2	teaspoons freshly ground pepper

Toss the cheese with the flour in a bowl. Place a metal bowl over a saucepan filled with two inches of water. Bring the water to a boil over high heat. Reduce the heat to medium and pour the beer into the bowl. Stir in garlic and shallots using a fork. Cook for 30 seconds stirring constantly. Add half of the cheese and cook until the cheese is melted, stirring constantly. Continue adding cheese and stirring until cheese is completely melted. Fold in pepper.

CHEF'S NOTE: Do not add water to the cheese fondue. If it is too thick, add more beer. If it is too thin, add more cheese!

BREWER'S PAIRING: Equinox Night Ryder Munich Dunkel
This dark, rich and sweet German lager gives a smooth contrast to the sharpness of the cheddar cheese dish. Hints of dark fruit add a unique complexity, while the clean lager finish leaves you ready to keep on dipping into that fondue over and over!

JONAS PORTER
MILK CHOCOLATE FONDUE

COLLABORATION	EQUINOX BREWING Brewer, Jared Lyon
	THE MELTING POT Chef, Tim Downey

PREP TIME: 5 minutes
4-6 SERVINGS

8	ounces milk chocolate
2	tablespoons Equinox Jonas Porter

Place a metal bowl over a saucepan filled with two inches of water. Bring the water to a boil over high heat. Reduce to a simmer and add the chocolate, stirring until it is melted. Fold in beer.

CHEF'S NOTE: Once the beer is fully incorporated, remove from heat as to not burn the chocolate!

BREWER'S PAIRING: Equinox Jonas Porter
Such a luscious chocolate dessert fondue needed something equally as rich and delicious to complement all the mouthwatering flavors. Jonas Porter offers light burnt chocolate/toffee notes with a rich and robust malt backbone. This dark beer is a perfect mix for that dessert dish that you know you shouldn't eat, but you have to because it's just so good!

"IF A MAN DROPS A PIECE OF BREAD IN THE FONDUE, HE HAS TO BUY THE NEXT BOTTLE OF WINE. IF A LADY DROPS IT, SHE HAS TO KISS THE GUY ON THE RIGHT OR HOST THE NEXT FONDUE PARTY."

- TIM DOWNEY

"I FELL IN LOVE WITH BAKING AND WAS LITERALLY HOOKED WHEN I WAS THREE YEARS OLD AND ACCIDENTLY GOT STUCK IN THE MIXER. SINCE THEN, I HAVEN'T BEEN ABLE TO STOP."

- JEAN CLAUDE

SPACE GHOST IPA BEER CREPES

COLLABORATION

EQUINOX BREWING Brewer, Jared Lyon
LA CREPERIE & FRENCH BAKERY OF FORT COLLINS Chef, Jean Claude

PREP TIME: 15 minutes
SERVES: 15 crepes

4	eggs		6½	ounces sugar
4	ounces milk		1	tablespoon vanilla
1	(12 ounce) bottle Equinox Space Ghost IPA		1	tablespoon rum
			1	pound flour
1	pinch of salt			

1 Mix together eggs, milk, salt, sugar, vanilla and rum.

2 Mix in the flour. Once mixed, add the Space Ghost IPA.

3 Heat up pan, then add in a little butter and oil.

4 Put your crepe batter in pan, let sit for 40 seconds on one side and then 20 seconds on the other or until golden brown.

CHEF'S NOTE: If you want to experiment with filling, right after you flip the crepe you could add in some egg, cheese, turkey, or ham for a savory option. For a sweet option, enjoy whipped cream, strawberries, or Nutella. Get creative and have fun!

BREWER'S PAIRING: Equinox Dunkelweizen or Space Ghost

If you add in Nutella, I'd suggest using Dunkelweizen. If you use whipped cream and strawberries, try a stout. If you decide to go savory ham and cheese, use an American Style IPA or Space Ghost.

PATEROS CREEK BREWING COMPANY

established 2011

Nick Chase PATEROS CREEK BREWING COMPANY

Andrew Tuin BISETTI'S RESTAURANT

Nate Hines THE WELSH RABBIT CHEESE BISTRO

PATEROS CREEK BREWING
COMPANY COLLABORATIONS

BISETTI'S ITALIAN RESTAURANT *and*
THE WELSH RABBIT BISTRO

NICK CHASE, PATEROS CREEK BREWING COMPANY

Dreaming of days of sunshine and mountains, Nick and his wife packed their bags and moved from New York to Colorado. Upon their arrival, Nick discovered the art of home brewing and decided to hang up his chef's hat of eight years. "Something clicked with brewing—it's like cooking, but a little more relaxing. You can spend all day experimenting and when it's done, it is delicious." Eager to jump into the brewing scene, he joined a home brewing club in the community, and befriended Steve, a local brewery owner of Pateros Creek Brewing. Steve gave Nick an opportunity to shadow him. Soon after, Nick wanted to help the brewery expand so he invested in canning equipment and later became the first paid employee at the brewery. As a brewer, Nick often combines his hobbies of music and the arts by brewing selective beers for local musicians and museum features. In honor of the reintroduction of the black-footed ferret to Northern Colorado, Nick developed the delicious Prairie Bandit Ale with flavors of fresh baked bread accented by fruity notes.

ANDREW TUIN, BISETTI'S ITALIAN RESTAURANT

Chef Andrew Tulin initiated his culinary career in 2001 at Bisetti's Italian Ristorante (a legendary Italian landmark in Old Town Fort Collins) and has been there for almost a decade. "I had originally planned on getting my engineering degree from CSU, but found myself a natural in the art of food and the culinary industry." Fusing the new world recipes with the old, particularly with beer, is Andrew's latest specialty. "I like the versatility of cooking with beer because there are a variety of beers and so many different flavors. It's a new unfamiliar element and a challenge." When approached with a task to create a tiramisu cooked with beer, he gladly accepted. He transformed an ordinary tiramisu to a beerlicious masterpiece, which he now refers to as Beeramisu. When he feels the urge to create his favorite dish, he will most likely be steaming up some seriously saucy mussels. "They are so much fun to cook. I like the sound of them clanking around in the pan. Then I love to add in my secret spicy red sauce recipe!" When not cooking, his guilty pleasure is salted caramel cheesecake. "Every morning, I eat cheesecake for breakfast. After preparing salted caramel cheesecakes at the restaurant, I have to taste it of course… so I end up eating the entire piece," laughs Andrew.

NATE HINES, THE WELSH RABBIT BISTRO

"As a child I wanted to be three things: a cook, a cowboy, and Luke Skywalker. By Halloween, I will have accomplished all three." A Texas native, Nate, moved to Synder to fulfill the cowboy dream when he was 18 years old. "I spent days in the saddle at a ranch dreaming about cooking so I went to culinary school at Cordon Bleu, in Portland, Oregon." His first interest in school was discovering about the versatility of salt. In his classes, he tasted everything from typical kinds of salt to reindeer antler salt. He also realized how much of a food geek he was. "School got me going into this great fun geeky world. I love being a food geek!" After culinary school, Nate began working at a five star hunting ranch, where he learned about cooking wild game. In 2011, Nate moved to Fort Collins to help his family open Welsh Rabbit Cheese Shop. Being a part of the cheese shop was such an adrenaline rush for Nate, he decided to open his very own bistro. He designed The Welsh Rabbit Bistro for locals to have a quaint place for a glass of wine and a small appetizer. Nate also encourages people to come in and bring their adventurous appetite and sample some of his tapas that are difficult to find elsewhere, like the polenta ostrich or bison tongue.

RIVERSIDE PASSION BEERAMISU

COLLABORATION | **PATEROS CREEK BREWING COMPANY** Brewer, Nick Chase
BISETTI'S ITALIAN RESTAURANT Chef, Andrew Tuin

PREP TIME: 35 minutes
REST: 30 minutes
10-12 SERVINGS

½	cup brewed coffee		⅛	cup amaretto liquor
1	Pateros Creek Riverside Passion		1	teaspoon vanilla extract
3	cups heavy whipping cream		30-40	ladyfingers
1¼	pound mascarpone cheese		½	cup chocolate shavings
¾	cup sugar		1	teaspoon cocoa powder (optional)

1 Combine the cream, sugar, amaretto and vanilla extract in mixing bowl. Using an electric mixer, whisk on medium speed until cream begins to thicken up or form "soft peaks." Next add in the mascarpone cheese and mix on low speed until incorporated. Turn mixer speed up to medium high and continue to whisk until mixture becomes nice and fluffy and spreadable. Set aside.

2 In large casserole dish, evenly lay out the ladyfingers lengthwise, covering the entire bottom of the pan. In a measuring cup, combine the coffee and Riverside Passion beer. Pour half of this evenly over the ladyfingers. Allow the ladyfingers to soak up the liquid for one minute.

3 Next, using a spatula, evenly spread half of the cream mixture over the ladyfingers. Be careful when spreading the cream to not smash the ladyfingers as they will be soft from the liquid. Sprinkle half of the chocolate shavings evenly over the layer. Repeat this process with the remaining lady fingers, coffee and beer, and cream mixture, again allowing the ladyfingers to soak up the liquid before spreading out the cream.

4 Finish with evenly sprinkling the remaining chocolate shavings on the top. Also, evenly sprinkle the optional cocoa powder on top.

5 Place in refrigerator and allow to set for at least 30 minutes.

6 To serve, cut with a knife dipped in hot water wiping the blade after each cut to avoid it sticking to the knife.

CHEF'S NOTE: Chocolate shavings can be made using a vegetable peeler on a piece of chocolate. Or you can just chop the chocolate with a knife.

BREWER'S PAIRING: Pateros Creek Cache La Porter
The Porter has nice rich chocolate notes that pair well with the sweetness of the tiramisu.

RUSTIC RED FETTUCCINE BOLOGNESE WITH TOASTED BARLEY

COLLABORATION | **PATEROS CREEK BREWING COMPANY** Brewer, Nick Chase
BISETTI'S ITALIAN RESTAURANT Chef, Andrew Tuin

PREP TIME: 30 minutes
3-4 SERVINGS

1	pound Italian sausage		1	tablespoon olive oil
½	yellow onion, diced		1	bottle Pateros Creek Rustic Red
1	rib celery, diced		2-3	teaspoons caramel barley (available at Pateros Creek)
¾	teaspoon salt, kosher		½	teaspoon unsalted butter
⅛	teaspoon pepper		3-4	basil leaves, rough chopped
1	teaspoon fresh parsley, finely chopped		2-3	ounces fresh mozzarella
1	teaspoon fresh thyme, stems removed and finely chopped		8	ounces tomato paste
2	cups chicken stock		1	pound dried pasta (fettuccine)
1	teaspoon garlic, minced			

Sauté the onion, celery, and garlic in the olive oil. Cook on medium heat until the onions turn translucent. Add in the Italian sausage, and using a spoon, continuously break up the sausage to the desired size. Cook the sausage until almost done. Next add in the chicken stock, tomato paste, salt, pepper, parsley, thyme and Rustic Red beer. Stir until well incorporated. Bring to a boil, then reduce heat and simmer covered for 25-30 minutes.

Meanwhile, cook the dried pasta according to the directions on the package. Try to time it so the pasta and sauce are finished at the same time. While the pasta and sauce are cooking in small pan, lightly "toast" the caramel barley on low heat with butter. Cook it just enough to bring out the aroma of the barley, being careful not to burn as it will burn fast. To serve, place pasta in a bowl. Ladle or spoon sauce on top of the pasta. Sprinkle toasted barley on top, along with the chopped basil. Finish by placing fresh mozzarella on top.

CHEF'S NOTE: You may substitute any dried pasta for the fettuccine. If you are adventurous try making your own fresh pasta!

BREWER'S PAIRING: Pateros Creek Rustic Red
The Red has nice caramel and roasted barley notes that pair well with the sausage. The slightly sweet finish complements the tomato sauce.

ARTHUR'S RAUCH SALMON CHOWDER

COLLABORATION	PATEROS CREEK BREWING COMPANY Brewer, Nick Chase
	BISETTI'S ITALIAN RESTAURANT Chef, Andrew Tuin

PREP TIME: 45 minutes-1 hour
YIELDS 3 QUARTS

1	yellow onion, finely chopped	1-2	tablespoons salt, kosher
4	ribs celery, finely chopped	¼	teaspoon ground white pepper
1	large carrot, peeled and finely chopped	¼	teaspoon cayenne pepper
1	potato (russet), diced	2	teaspoons Worcestershire sauce
5	slices bacon	½	bay leaf
8	ounces salmon	3	tablespoons corn starch
2	quarts chicken stock	½	cup water
½	quart heavy cream	1	teaspoon olive oil
1	bottle Pateros Creek Arthur's Rauch		

1 In large saucepot sauté the onion, celery and carrot in the oil until the onions become translucent and the carrots are soft.

2 Dice potato and in separate pot cook in water until tender. Strain and reserve.

3 Next, cook 4 slices of bacon on either a baking sheet or sauté pan until done. Reserve one piece of bacon for flavoring the soup. Rough chop the cooked bacon and reserve.

4 Dice the salmon and season with a little salt and cayenne pepper. Cook on high heat in a little olive oil until just cooked through. Strain off any excess oil and reserve.

5 Now add the beer, cream and chicken stock to the vegetables in the saucepot. Bring to a boil and then reduce to a simmer. Then, add in the cooked bacon, the remaining slice of uncooked bacon, potatoes, salmon, bay leaf, Worcestershire sauce and remaining seasonings.

6 Continue to simmer for 20-30 minutes, skimming off any excess oil that comes to the top with a ladle.

7 Lastly, in small cup whisk the corn starch and water together to form a slurry. Bring soup back to a boil and slowly whisk in the corn starch mix until desired thickness is reached. Continue to boil for one minute to incorporate corn starch mix. Remove from heat immediately. As always taste the soup and adjust the salt seasoning to your liking.

CHEF'S NOTE: Make sure the soup is boiling before you add in the corn starch mix.

BREWER'S PAIRING: Pateros Creek Arthur's Rauch
The Rauch has a very distinctive smoked character to it that balances the rich creaminess of the chowder and accents the smokiness of the bacon.

SPENT GRAIN CHAPATTI

COLLABORATION	**PATEROS CREEK BREWING COMPANY** Brewer, Nick Chase **THE WELSH RABBIT CHEESE BISTRO** Chef, Nate Hines

PREP TIME: 30 minutes
12 SERVINGS

4	cups flour		3	tablespoons olive oil
1	cup spent grain		1½	cups Pateros Creek Old Town Ale
3	teaspoons salt			

Toss the flour and spent grain into a mixing bowl fitted with a dough hook. With the mixer running on low, add in the salt and olive oil. Slowly add the beer until the dough pulls away from the side of the bowl and starts to "climb" up the bread hook. Depending on how damp the spent grains are, it could be as little as ¾ cup and as much as 1½ cups. Continue to knead until the dough is barely tacky to the touch. Remove from bowl and cover for at least 15 minutes to rest (gluten, much like me, likes little breaks to relax).

Cut dough into four-ounce portions and roll out until roughly ⅙ of an inch thick. Traditionally the shape is a circle but we tend to go more of an oval shape just purely for the reason our plates tend to be rectangular. Heat a pan over a medium flame and coat lightly with olive oil. Cook the dough until air pockets start to puff, then flip and cook for one minute more. Remove and keep warm. Drizzle with balsamic. We tend to smother these in shredded cheese and toss them in the oven until melted, but much like flat breads around the world—the possibilities are pretty much only limited by your imagination.

CHEF'S NOTE: If you are lucky enough to know a home brewer or be near a small brewery like we are, then this is a lovely way to use up some of the spent grain from the brewing process.

BREWER'S PAIRING: Pateros Creek Old Town Ale
A crisp refreshing light bodied beer that cuts the richness of the chapatti and accents the floral sweetness of the balsamic.

"I LOVE CHEESE! I SEIZE ANY BEER AND CHEESE PAIRING OPPORTUNITIES I CAN FIND. AT THE END OF THE DAY, I'M ADDICTED. I DON'T CARE WHAT CHEESE I EAT; I'LL TRY ANYTHING. I DON'T KNOW IF IT'S A TEXTURE THING OR DAIRY—I JUST LOVE IT. A MATCH MADE IN HEAVEN."

- NICK CHASE

WELSH RABBIT SALAD

COLLABORATION | **PATEROS CREEK BREWING COMPANY** Brewer, Nick Chase
THE WELSH RABBIT CHEESE BISTRO Chef, Nate Hines

PREP TIME: 8 minutes
7 SERVINGS

5	tablespoons olive oil		salt
¼	cup onions, minced		fresh cracked pepper
1	cup Pateros Creek Old Town Ale	35	rye croutons
3	tablespoons white balsamic	7	ounces powerful Welsh cheddar
4	tablespoons honey	5¼	cups lettuce of choice
2	tablespoons mustard		

Combine onions, Old Town Ale, vinegar, honey, mustard, salt and pepper into a blender and run on high until fully incorporated. Slowly (and by slowly, I mean think of molasses in January) add in the olive oil to create an emulsification. Place lettuce on the plate. To hearken back to the original spirit of the recipe, drizzle a little mustard dressing on the lettuce and place the croutons and cheddar on top.

CHEF'S NOTE: From this point on it is all a matter of preference. I find that the dressing flavor comes out more if the salad is tossed, but the mustard we use causes for a yellow dressing that pops quite nice. With that in mind we lightly dress the salad and use the "extra" to make whimsical patterns on the plate.

BREWER'S PAIRING: Pateros Creek Mt. Massive Imperial IPA
Aggressive bitterness accents the spiciness of the greens while cutting the richness of the cheese. The higher ABV helps you forget you're eating a salad.

MOUNT MASSIVE BUTTERMILK PIE

COLLABORATION	PATEROS CREEK BREWING COMPANY Brewer, Nick Chase
	THE WELSH RABBIT CHEESE BISTRO Chef, Nate Hines

PREP TIME: 40 minutes
6 SERVINGS

2	cups sugar	$\frac{2}{3}$	cup buttermilk
½	teaspoon salt	$\frac{1}{3}$	cup Pateros Creek Mount Massive
3	tablespoons polenta	1	(8 inch) piecrust
4	eggs	½	cup heavy cream
½	cup melted butter		

1 Preheat oven to 350°.

2 Place the sugar, salt and polenta in a large mixing bowl and stir briefly to combine. Whisk in the eggs one at a time, then stir in the melted butter, buttermilk and beer.

3 Pour the mixture into an uncooked pie shell (if we have done this right, you should have about ¾ of a cup left over) and bake for 25 to 30 minutes. This is that annoying part of the recipe where you have to give the pie a little shake and make a judgment call. I always think if it jiggles a little like my belly it is just about right.

4 While the pie is doing its thing in the oven, add the remaining buttermilk mixture to the heavy cream in a bowl and whisk over barely simmering water until thick. This will create a nice little sauce to cut the sweetness of the pie once it is ready to be served.

CHEF'S NOTE: I am a huge fan of adding a bit of whipped cream flavored with bourbon to top it off. Bourbon and beer is never a bad way to end a meal.

BREWER'S PAIRING: Pateros Creek Howe's it Hangin' IPA
This unique American IPA's tropical fruit notes will complement the richness of the polenta, while the bready malt body adds depth and character to the dish.

BLACK BOTTLE BREWERY

established 2012

Sean Nook **BLACK BOTTLE BREWERY**

Garrett Marlin **UNCLE'S PIZZERIA**

Russ Robinson **CHOICE CITY BUTCHER & DELI**

BLACK BOTTLE BREWERY COLLABORATIONS

UNCLE'S PIZZERIA *and*
CHOICE CITY BUTCHER & DELI

SEAN NOOK, BLACK BOTTLE BREWERY

Sean Nook grew up in Fort Collins and was utterly spoiled by great beer. Inspired by the trendy breweries that surrounded him, he began to explore home brewing. "I soon became passionate about brewing and latched onto it." His determination to continue creating craft brews influenced him to quit his job as a mechanic and pursue brewing full time. "I'm extremely stubborn and wanted to prove to myself that I could start my own brewery. After a lot of hard work and many sleepless nights, I opened Black Bottle Brewery." According to Sean, his brewery is one of the first in Fort Collins to offer other local beers on tap as well as his own creations. "We have great beer and are community based. We support other breweries, not just our own. There are 15-20 of our own beers on tap, and just as many or more of guest taps." Sean designed the brewery to be different than the ordinary. When walking into the taproom, his blunt sense of humor and sarcastic nature is reflected throughout. Sean easily captures his guests' attention with his edgy beer names such as Scuba Steve, and colorful signs, like the one above the diaper changing tables: "Please do not drop your child—Thanks, Management." Sean's playful personality is also showcased through his stuffed squirrels placed above the taps as well as his shamelessly funny YouTube videos he creates with his staff. "We love to make fun of people and each other while embracing our weirdness." Sean's mission is to create unique handcrafted lagers and ales. He surely succeeded when he caught the attention of beer enthusiasts all around the world with his cereal concept brew Count Chocula!

GARRETT MARLIN, UNCLE'S PIZZERIA

For Chef Garrett Marlin, it was love at first pizza. Somewhere between tossing pizzas with his mom as a child and working at a pizza parlor in Hawaii, he was hooked. "Creating pizzas became something I love to do." In 2006, Garrett and his father, Dennis established Uncle's Pizzeria bringing an "old school Italian flavor with a twist" to Fort Collins. They quickly turned a small neighborhood pizza place into a Fort Collins staple. Delicious hand-tossed east coast pizzas and fresh homemade Italian pastas are offered at this local family favorite. "We make house and custom pizzas that range from straight forward to seasonally inspired pizzas. In our open kitchen, you can see pizzas being tossed and great cocktails or local beers being poured at the bar." Garrett continues to perfect his pizza skills by entering pizza-tossing contests in New York, competing with the top pizza chefs around the world. In 2012, he won the World's Best Pizza Stretcher and is determined to bring home another trophy soon. When Garrett isn't tossing ginormous pizzas, he is most likely spending time with his wife and two children. "We love to ride our bikes to the park, chase our dog, and act silly."

RUSS ROBINSON, CHOICE CITY BUTCHER & DELI

Directly after Russ's final exams at Ohio State, he got into his car and headed towards Vail, Colorado to become a ski bum. En route to Vail, he landed in Fort Collins to visit a friend. Russ quickly fell in love with the community and decided to call Fort Collins his new home. In 2007, he established Choice City Butcher and Deli, providing the community with a neighborhood butcher and deli shop. He explains, "I wanted to put the butcher back into buying meat again. 11 years ago, grocery stores were taking over butcher shops. As a child, I was inspired by the character Sam the Butcher in The Brady Brunch, who provided personal service to customers. I try and do the same and offer my guests cooking tips for the meat they purchase." Russ serves a variety of custom deli sandwiches for breakfast, lunch and dinner. "Our butcher shop has specialty meats from kangaroo to pork belly, so we can put together specials that no one else can because they are at our finger tips." One of his biggest sellers is a sausage that is a combination of rabbit, rattlesnake, jalapeño, and chardonnay. While enjoying one of his scrumptious specialty sandwiches, customers can choose a beer from his world-renowned beer menu (#9 on the RateBeer list of best beer restaurants in the world for 2011). After almost a decade, Russ still remains quite passionate for food, beer, and people. He is grateful to be a part of the food scene. "I enjoy offering unbelievable beers and food. It feels like home here and I've always loved to give that back to the community."

"I WANTED TO PUT THE BUTCHER BACK INTO BUYING MEAT AGAIN."

- RUSS ROBINSON

CARLOS' RICOTTA GNOCCHI

| COLLABORATION | BLACK BOTTLE BREWERY Brewer, Sean Nook | UNCLE'S PIZZERIA Chef, Garrett Martin |

PREP TIME: 10 minutes
COOKING THE DISH: 6-8 minutes, making the pan sauce: 3-5 minutes
4 SERVINGS

RICOTTA GNOCCHI

7	ounces all purpose flour		2	tablespoons butter (unsalted)
8	ounces ricotta cheese		1	cup mushrooms with vegetables
3	egg yolks		1	pinch each red pepper flakes, kosher salt, pepper
1	ounce parmesan cheese		½	cup Black Bottle Carlos
1	pinch each pepper, kosher salt, nutmeg		¼	cup pasta water

SAUCE

2	tablespoons canola oil		4	tablespoons heavy cream

Weigh out all gnocchi ingredients and mix them until combined in a bowl. Divide the dough into four pieces. Roll each piece into a log just smaller than one inch in diameter. After you have formed the logs cut each log into half inch pieces. Lightly dust the gnocchi with all-purpose flour and then repeat, cutting the other logs until you have cut all the dough into the gnocchi.

Fill a large bowl with ice water. The ice bath for the pasta will stop the cooking and allow the pasta to hold until assembly.

Bring a large pot of water to a gentle boil. The water should not be at a roiling boil. You are really poaching the pasta not boiling the heck out of it. Salt your water and then in three batches cook the pasta until it floats to the surface. Scoop out and place directly in ice bath.

In a sauté pan, heat the oil and butter on medium heat. Sauté cut mushrooms until brown. Add spices, then add beer and reduce the liquid by half. Add the water and cream. Reduce until the pasta sauce thickens to a syrup consistency. Add the pasta and cook uncovered for about three minutes until the pasta is heated through.

CHEF'S NOTE: Feel free to use the pasta sauce as a base. Use whatever vegetables and spices you want. Maybe add some lemon zest, mint and basil. It's your dinner, use what you like.

BREWER'S PAIRING: Black Bottle Carlos Liquid Metal
Dry-hopped Carlos soul cooked little Gnocchis. Tastes so good it will make you want to slap your MAMA. After all that please share a Liquid Metal and these Gnocchis with her to say sorry...

DEEP DISH GRANDMA PIZZA

COLLABORATION	BLACK BOTTLE BREWERY Brewer, Sean Nook	UNCLE'S PIZZERIA Chef, Garrett Martin

PREP TIME: 10 minutes to knead and mix dough
30-45 minutes for first dough rise, 30-45 minutes for second dough rise
COOKING THE DOUGH: 15-20 minutes, cooking the pizza with toppings: 10-15 minutes
3-5 SERVINGS

DOUGH

17	ounces bread flour
¼	cup ground barley/beer grain
7	ounces warm water
3	ounces Black Bottle Hipster IPA
½	tablespoon active dry yeast
½	ounce salt
1	tablespoon sugar
½	ounce extra virgin olive oil

TOPPING

1	cup pizza/tomato sauce
12	ounces whole milk mozzarella (low moisture)
	handful of kalamata olives
	handful of pancetta
¼	cup halved cherry tomatoes
¼	cup caramelized onions
½	tablespoon red pepper flakes
	fresh basil

Weigh out all dough ingredients first. Place flour, grains, yeast, sugar and salt in a large bowl. Mix all dry ingredients well, and then make a well in the center of flour mixture. Add the water and oil and mix well with wooden spoon until combined. Scrape out onto a board, knead, slap and punch for ten minutes total. It will be really wet, don't add extra flour. Mix for five minutes, then let the dough rest for five minutes and then finish the kneading. Roll into a large ball. The dough after a short rest should knead easily and be silky smooth.

Clean out bowl you used prior, coat with a bit of olive oil, place dough ball seam side down, cover with plastic wrap and let double in size. Then get the largest brownie pan you can find. We use a hotel pan (20" x 12") at the restaurant.

Oil generously with olive oil, flip dough out into pan and press into all the edges and corners. Place plastic wrap over the pan and let rise again until it doubles in size.

Place in the oven at 500° and bake until golden brown on top. About 15 minutes. Pull out and let cool in the pan until it gets to room temperature or at least 30 minutes if you don't have time.

Place cheese evenly over dough, then spoon sauce over cheese. Don't worry about covering all the cheese. The cheese and sauce should be "patchy." Then place your pizza toppings on top of the pizza and bake in the oven for another 15 minutes. Reserve the basil for after the pizza is finished baking. Let rest for five minutes before cutting, otherwise the toppings will skid off the top of the pizza. If you don't have a pizza cutter just use a big chef's knife on a cutting board.

CHEF'S NOTE: Don't use all-purpose flour for the pizza because you will get dough that's not as chewy as you might think. But use all-purpose flour if that's all you have.

BREWER'S PAIRING: Black Bottle Hipster IPA
Hipster IPA infused Deep dish Pizza, with sooooo much flavor-flav, it is good enough for any type of HIPSTER.

"SEAN IS ONE FUN BREWER. ANYONE THAT KNOWS HIM AND WATCHES HIS CREATIVE YOUTUBE VIDEOS WOULD AGREE. COLLABORATING WITH HIM BROUGHT OUT MY PLAYFUL SIDE."

- RUSS ROBINSON

HIPSTER BRUSSEL SPROUTS

| COLLABORATION | **BLACK BOTTLE BREWERY** Brewer, Sean Nook |
| | **CHOICE CITY BUTCHER & DELI** Chef, Russ Robinson |

PREP TIME: 10 minutes
4-6 SERVINGS

1   pound brussel sprouts, cut in half lengthwise

6   slices bacon, chopped ¼ inch pieces

2   portabella caps, chopped ½ inch pieces

½   red onion, chopped ¼ inch pieces

1   growler (64 ounces) Black Bottle Hipster IPA

First things first, pour you and your guests a Black Bottle Brewery Hipster IPA. In a large skillet cook bacon over medium-high heat until nice and greasy (about five minutes), add red onion, stir and caramelize (one minute). Add brussel sprouts (it's ok that the sprouts come apart), stir and cook until almost done (about 10 minutes). At this point, pour yourself another Black Bottle Brewery Hipster IPA and enjoy.

Add mushrooms, stir and cook two minutes. Pour half your pint of Black Bottle Hipster IPA in the skillet and cook for another minute or two. Plate and serve.

CHEF'S NOTE: My beer and food pairing philosophy is that good beer goes with good food.

BREWER'S PAIRING: Black Bottle Hipster IPA
Two Hipsters, KILLER IPA, Bacon, mustache = DUHHH!!!!

1933 BREWING COMPANY

established 2013

Zach Wilson 1933 BREWING COMPANY

Joel Ryan THE KITCHEN

Justin Burdick THE MAINLINE ALE HOUSE

1933 BREWING COMPANY COLLABORATIONS

THE KITCHEN *and*
THE MAINLINE ALE HOUSE

ZACH WILSON, 1933 BREWING COMPANY

Zach is an innovative, laid-back brewer and sizzles with creativity. At an early age, he was introduced to home brewing by his father. While studying environmental science at the University of Hawaii, Zach became fascinated with the connection between chemistry and brewing. This interest led him to pursue brewing full time. "I've always liked to work with my hands and create things—I'm a potter and woodworker—but brewing was the first hands on project where I didn't get burnt out." After Zach graduated, he accepted his first job as an assistant brewer at Nui Mehana Brewery in Hawaii. During this time, he embraced the island life, experimented with brewing, and surfed. A few years later he moved to Colorado and became the head brewer of 1933 Brewing. Zach prefers to offer a variety of beers. "I try and develop flagship beers, but also brew what people ask for. We don't have a specific style so we are able to offer English, French, American, Scottish, and Irish beers. I love to experiment with crazy beers. Right now, I'm working on a funky squash saison flavored with local grown squash and spices from Old Town Spice Shop." Outside of developing these creative brews, Zach enjoys making pottery, playing guitar with his lovely girlfriend Laura, and hunting. He is also a very talented woodworker and designed the hand-carved wooden taps at the brewery.

JOEL RYAN, THE KITCHEN

Joel Ryan is one talented chef and brings a fresh culinary contribution to the community by embracing the local farm to table movement. His dedication to this movement originates from his childhood. "I grew up on a cattle ranch in southern Oklahoma. Good food was always around. Whether it was garden vegetables, native pecans, or my family's own beef, we always had fresh food on the table. One of my earliest memories was going to a neighbor's farm with my grandmother to get raw milk and butcher wild game and fish. Those early sensory experiences still serve as a guide as I strive to maintain the integrity of the local, seasonal ingredients I use in my own cooking." As an executive chef at The Kitchen, Joel continues this community mindset by building a direct, in-depth relationship with four local farmers. "The farmers are my friends, and we are super close. Supporting local producers, respecting what they do and the products they provide is important to me. It's not about what I want, it's about how we can work together." Joel also enjoys applying this fresh food concept to his passion for hunting, fishing, and simply being immersed in the outdoors. Quite often, he cooks his daily catch outside over an open flame. It is easy to see that fresh food simply prepared is almost always a recipe for success for chef Joel.

JUSTIN BURDICK, THE MAINLINE ALE HOUSE

"The Dalai Lama says, 'Approach both food and love with reckless abandon.' This quote hits home for me because it's true. You put yourself out there—just like with someone you love, it's the same with food. This makes sense for me and my cooking." At the age of 25, Justin realized his calling to be a chef. The feeling of being under pressure and the constant adrenaline rush are aspects of cooking that Justin thrives off of. After completing culinary school, he moved to Las Vegas and studied under several prestigious chefs including Wolfgang Puck, and Mark Sandoval. "In three months of working for them, I learned more than I did in my three years of culinary school. They taught me how to be patient with others and myself. I cooked for celebrities including Tim Allen, 50 Cent, and Steve Wynn." Justin returned to his home state, Colorado and became the executive chef at the Mainline. He designs dishes that the community enjoys by offering contemporary American cuisine. Justin is always looking for ways to expand his knowledge of food. "Food can be exciting, colorful, fresh, and challenging. I like to learn something new everyday while I'm cooking. One of my favorite activities is going to the Farmer's Market every Saturday. I find unique vegetables or fruits and come up with new dishes. I recently bought a finger lime, which has pearl-like jewels inside that I threw into a ceviche creation. I also discovered a tomato that looks like a banana and is six inches long—we'll see where that leads me!" Outside of finding peculiar produce, Justin loves to go camping and fishing.

"ZACH IS AN EQUALLY PASSIONATE GUY. WE HAVE THE SAME VIEWPOINTS ON ETHICS, QUALITY AND COMMUNITY. I THINK THAT'S WHY WE HIT IT OFF. WE STILL GET TOGETHER AND TALK ABOUT DOING ANOTHER COLLABORATION."

- JOEL RYAN

MUSSELS WITH 1933 MAIBOCK, CHORIZO AND FENNEL

COLLABORATION | **1933 BREWING COMPANY** Brewer, Zach Wilson   **THE KITCHEN** Chef, Joel Ryan

PREP TIME: 30 minutes
YIELDS 1 QUART

1	quart mussels, cleaned
1	cup of 1933 Maibock
2	inch piece Spanish chorizo, thinly sliced
¼	cup fennel bulb, thinly sliced
2	cloves garlic, thinly sliced
2	tablespoons shallot, finely diced

1	teaspoon Fresno chile, seeded and finely diced
¼	teaspoon orange zest, grated
1	tablespoon extra virgin olive oil
2	tablespoons unsalted butter
½	teaspoon salt

Heat a medium sized, heavy-bottomed saucepan over medium high heat. Add the olive oil, then chorizo. Allow the chorizo to render briefly, then add the next five ingredients. Sauté for one minute, add the mussels and stir. Immediately add the Maibock and cook until the mussels begin to open.

Once all mussels have opened use a slotted spoon to transfer them to a serving bowl. Add butter to the liquid remaining in the pan and continue cooking and stirring until the butter is incorporated. Add salt, stir briefly and pour hot sauce over the mussels. Garnish with fennel frond and serve with grilled bread.

CHEF'S NOTE: Always purchase the highest quality mussels from a reputable source. Gently tap any open fresh mussels, if they don't close discard them.

BREWER'S PAIRING: 1933 Maibock or Oatmeal Stout

If you like sweet and savory dishes, the Maibock is a smart choice. The Belgian candy sugar and honey notes of the Maibock will pair well. If you're going for hearty and savory, the Oatmeal Stout would be nice. The heartiness and roasted character of the Oatmeal Stout pairs really well with a light yet savory dish such as mussels.

1933 OATMEAL STOUT ICE CREAM

COLLABORATION | **1933 BREWING COMPANY** Brewer, Zach Wilson   **THE KITCHEN** Chef, Joel Ryan

ACTIVE PREP TIME: 1½ hours
YIELDS 3 PINTS

2½	cups 1933 Oatmeal Stout	1	cup heavy cream
1	cup rolled oats	1¼	cups granulated sugar
½	cup golden raisins	6	egg yolks
5	cups whole milk	1	tablespoon vanilla paste

In a small bowl, combine the oats and raisins. Add the Oatmeal Stout and stir to combine. Cover the bowl with plastic wrap and let stand at room temperature for one hour.

Strain the oatmeal/beer mixture through a fine mesh strainer, reserving the liquid. In a heavy saucepan, heat the milk, cream, vanilla and half the sugar over medium-high heat until it reaches a soft boil or 180°.

Meanwhile in a medium bowl, whisk the remaining sugar with the egg yolks. When the milk mixture reaches 180°, temper it into the eggs.

Return the mix to the saucepan and add the liquid from the beer/oatmeal/raisin mixture, whisking to combine. Continue to cook on low heat, stirring constantly until the base thickens slightly.

Strain this ice cream base into a sealable container and chill overnight. Proceed according to your ice cream manufacturer's directions.

CHEF'S NOTE: My pastry chef, Cully Eisner-Terrill developed this recipe. She suggests serving it "affogato" style by pouring a shot of espresso or stout beer over the ice cream.

BREWER'S PAIRING: 1933 Oatmeal Stout
The bready and biscuity characteristic you get from the Oatmeal Stout, not to mention the creaminess, really balances out a nice ice cream. It makes for a smooth ice cream cocktail.

THE MAINLINE BROWN ALE BACON BURGER & BACON JAM

COLLABORATION	1933 BREWING COMPANY Brewer, Zach Wilson
	THE MAINLINE ALE HOUSE Chef, Justin Burdick

BROWN ALE BACON JAM

PREP TIME: 20 minutes
12 SERVINGS (2 OUNCE)

½	pound bacon, diced	2	cups brown sugar
3	red onion, diced	3	tablespoons balsamic vinegar
2	cups 1933 Brown Ale		

1 Put bacon in pot on medium-high heat.

2 Once cooked half way, add diced red onion, cook on medium heat.

3 Once onions are soft and translucent, add Brown Ale and brown sugar.

4 Let cook until the Brown Ale is reduced by half, then add balsamic vinegar.

5 Blend until smooth and let cool.

MAINLINE BROWN ALE BURGER

PREP TIME: 20 minutes
12 SERVINGS (2 OUNCE)

½	pound ground chuck	1	slice red onion
1	Kaiser roll	3	ounces Brown Ale Bacon Jam
1	leaf lettuce		pinch salt
1	slice tomato		pinch black pepper

1 Season ground chuck with salt and pepper.

2 Hand form patty and cook to desired temperature.

3 Top with Brown Ale Bacon Jam, lettuce, tomatoes and onion.

4 Serve on buttered and toasted kaiser roll.

CHEF'S NOTE: This is an amazing combination of smoky flavors with the brown ale bacon jam. Perfect for summer time barbeque.

BREWER'S PAIRING: 1933 Brown Ale

Brown Ale and burgers. What's better than that?

GOLDEN ALE DIJON CITRUS SALAD

COLLABORATION | **1933 BREWING COMPANY** Brewer, Zach Wilson
THE MAINLINE ALE HOUSE Chef, Justin Burdick

GOLDEN ALE DIJON CITRUS SALAD

PREP TIME: 12 minutes
1 SERVING

½	cup grape fruit segments		pinch salt	
½	cup orange segments		pinch black pepper	
¼	cup strawberries	2	ounces Sweet Golden Ale Dijon	
¼	cup grapes, halved	¼	ounce goat cheese	
4	ounces mixed greens			

1 In a large mixing bowl, combine all ingredients but cheese, mix well.
2 Garnish with cheese.

CHEF'S NOTE: This is a beautiful light salad with an amazing amount of flavor and color. High in citrus, but balanced with the richness of goat cheese. Use the dressing sparingly, for this salad does not need much. Enjoy!

SWEET GOLDEN ALE DIJON

PREP TIME: 10-15 minutes
YIELDS 24 OUNCES

1	shallot, diced	1	teaspoon parsley, chopped
¼	cup honey		pinch salt
½	cup 1933 Golden Ale		pinch white pepper
1	tablespoon dijon mustard	2	cups blended oil

1 In large mixing bowl, place mustard, shallot, parsley and half of Golden Ale.
2 Mix until all is incorporated, then add honey and mix.
3 While mixing, add oil in a slow constant stream. Mix until emulsified.
4 Once dressing has emulsified, add salt and pepper to taste.
5 Add water to adjust desired consistency.

CHEF'S NOTE: An emulsion is a mixture of two or more liquids that are normally non-mixable. In this case it would be the blended oil with the mixture of beer and honey. When mixing it is imperative that you have a consistent flow of oil, slow and steady.

BREWER'S PAIRING: 1933 Golden Ale
There's comradery between the cereal maltiness, light citrus hop notes of blonde ale, and the spicy and tart characteristics of the salad. This eliminates the competition between your beer and the lightness of the salad.

SNICKERDOODLE CRUST

COLLABORATION	1933 BREWING COMPANY Brewer, Zach Wilson
	THE MAINLINE ALE HOUSE
	Chef, Justin Burdick

PREP TIME: 1 hour
YIELDS 1 CRUST

1	cup butter, softened
1½	cups sugar
2	medium eggs
3	cups flour
¼	teaspoon fine salt
2	teaspoons ground cinnamon

1 Preheat oven to 350°. In a large bowl, combine the butter and sugar, and mix thoroughly with an electric mixer.
2 Add the eggs and mix thoroughly until creamy and well combined. Scrape bowl until dry.
3 In separate mixing bowl, sift together the flour, cream of tartar and salt.
4 Once sifted, stir dry mix into wet mixture.
5 Once dough is ready, cut into two equal pieces, wrap and chill for 30 minutes.
6 Dust with flour and roll out.
7 Press into buttered and floured pie pans.
8. Chill for 15 minutes.
9 Bake at 350°.

CHEF'S NOTE: These crusts are some of my favorites! The possibilities are endless when it comes time to decide how to fill them. Take your time when baking these; a little TLC makes all the difference when it comes to baking.

1933 OATMEAL STOUT CHOCOLATE GANACHE

COLLABORATION	1933 BREWING COMPANY Brewer, Zach Wilson
	THE MAINLINE ALE HOUSE
	Chef, Justin Burdick

PREP TIME: 30 minutes
        24 hours cooling
YIELDS 2 PIES

2	pounds bittersweet chocolate wafers
2	cups heavy cream
¾	cup 1933 Oatmeal Stout
½	cup corn syrup
2	snicker doodle piecrusts

1 Combine corn syrup and sugar with ¼ cup of water.

2 In a non-reactive pot cook until medium amber color. Watch closely and do not let crystalize!

3 Combine heavy cream and beer, and then steep. Do not boil.

4 Once hot, pour over chocolate, mix until smooth and all is incorporated.

5 Let sit for five to 10 minutes, then pour into snicker doodle piecrust and chill for 24 hours before serving.

CHEF'S NOTE: Cooling is essential! So please be patient! This dessert is a hit for any chocolate lover out there. With rich creamy chocolate and the nuttiness of the oatmeal stout, how could you go wrong? Enjoy!

BREWER'S PAIRING: 1933 Oatmeal Stout
Once you go sweet and stout, you never go back.

e Ale   5.6%

ale Ale   5.8%

IPA   7%

ge   7%

k IPA 6.2%

out   5.1%

FREEDOM'S EDGE BREWING COMPANY

established 2014

Adam Niebling & Shane Carson FREEDOM'S EDGE BREWING COMPANY

Aaron Conkey RIO GRANDE MEXICAN RESTAURANT

Stefanie, Patrick and Katie O'Neil VERN'S TOFFEE HOUSE

FREEDOM'S EDGE BREWING COMPANY COLLABORATIONS

ADAM NIEBLING AND SHANE CARSON, FREEDOM'S EDGE BREWING COMPANY

Brothers-in-law, Shane and Adam not only married their dream wives, but also gained a great friendship with each other. Their mutual interest for brewing became something they explored together. "We always liked beer and brewing. It's a very relaxing process and you can take your time—all you need is patience. Once we started making really good beer, we had to share it," explains Adam. In 2014, Freedom's Edge Brewing was established and they began their brewery adventures. Their focus is to brew great craft beer for the community. They offer eight beers on tap, two of which are their flagship brews (1890 IPA with citrus and grapefruit aromas, and their High Noon Chili Ale infused with jalapeño, habanero, and serrano peppers) and the rest are constantly changing to keep their customers guessing. This family run brewery has its perks for Adam, as he loves to spend time with his little one Aiden. According to Adam, Aiden knows more about the brewery equipment than most do. "We have some great father son bonding time. We play super heroes all the time. He has his little mask and I have mine, and we run around the brewery and chase the bad guys." Shane also spends time with his family's newest addition Carson, and likes to paint when he can.

AARON CONKEY, RIO GRANDE MEXICAN RESTAURANT

Aaron has a smile as big as his heart. He has a great love for not only food, but also his Rio family. The employees are his biggest priority while managing the kitchen of The Rio Grande. "The most important part of my job is making the kitchen staff into a family. I love my people. My care for my employees is the biggest reason I work here. I believe in them and want to give them opportunities so they can reach their full potential." Aaron often acts as a mentor for his staff as he encourages them to excel and gain knowledge of the various roles in the kitchen. Aaron's inner Boy Scout and anthropology degree also feed nicely into his leadership role as an executive chef. "My background as an Eagle Scout helps me as I lead and develop a team of people with 12 diverse cultural, social, and economic backgrounds." Everyday Aaron strives to reach out to his staff and help them feel valued and appreciated. At the end of his workday, he makes an effort to show gratitude to each of his employees. Outside of the kitchen, he is in his element when outdoors digging a hole and smoking a pig. He also appreciates his family time with his wife and new little one.

STEFANIE, PATRICK AND KATIE O'NEILL, VERN'S TOFFEE HOUSE

When you enter Vern's Toffee House, prepare yourself, as you are about to take in the most divine smells of cooking butter, sugar, roasted almonds, and chocolate. You will be greeted by the friendliest smiles in town, and taste delicious handcrafted creamy butter almond toffee that melts in your mouth and hooks you for life. The creators behind these pieces of heaven come from three generations of toffee makers, dating back to 1976. Currently, the joyful toffee makers and owners, Patrick, Stephanie, and their sweet daughter Katie are committed to making the best toffee you've ever had. They prepare it with lots of love, care, and a genuine heart for others. "It's the happiest place in the world! We have great toffee, positive people, and strive to make perfect candy through the process," says Patrick. Aside from producing exceptional toffee, Patrick and Stephanie value their customers and have a way of warming their hearts. "Customers are the most important people to us. If they have a story to tell me, I take the time to listen. That's why I'm here—to take care of them. I'll stand there for three hours if they want to talk. That's what we do—make them feel welcome and at home." With their delightful toffee and loving nature, it makes sense that Vern's Toffee House has been named one of the best places to visit in Fort Collins (Yahoo Travel) along with the best locally produced food product in town (Fort Collins Weekly).

"ONCE WE STARTED MAKING REALLY GOOD BEER, WE HAD TO SHARE IT."

- SHANE CARSON

1890 PORK CARNITAS & HIGH NOON CHILI ALE SLAW

COLLABORATION	FREEDOM'S EDGE BREWING COMPANY Brewer, Adam Niebling & Shane Carson
	RIO GRANDE MEXICAN RESTAURANT Chef, Aaron Conkey

1890 PORK CARNITAS

PREP TIME: 30 minutes
COOK TIME: 2.5 hours
4-6 SERVINGS

2	pounds boneless pork shoulder, cut into 2 inch pieces (leave the fat cap on)		4	fluid ounces orange juice
8	ounces Freedom's Edge Brewing 1890 IPA		4	fluid ounces water
2	tablespoons minced garlic		2	dried guajillo chiles (or 1 tablespoon of a mild chili powder)
1	tablespoon salt		12	flour or corn tortillas

1 Roast guajillo chiles in the oven on broil until slightly brown, approximately two minutes. Remove chili stem and seeds and dice into a fine powder.

2 After processing the pork into two inch pieces, coat with the salt and guajillo chili powder. Bring seasoned pork, beer, garlic, orange juice, and water to a boil in a pot. Make sure liquid level in the cooking vessel covers the pork. Cover, reduce heat, and simmer until pork is fork tender (60-80 minutes).

3 Uncover pork and turn heat to high. Slowly reduce the liquid mixture and gently rotate pork pieces until they become brown on the outside. Be careful not to simply stir the pork around or you will begin to shred it instead of caramelizing the pieces. 10-15 minutes.

4 Heat tortillas in the oven under a towel, in the microwave, or in a pan depending on preference. Place pork carnitas inside and serve.

CHEF'S NOTE: Carnitas are not supposed to be shredded; keep the pieces whole by turning, not stirring, as you are caramelizing the beer and orange juice reduction around the pork. When reheating store bought corn or flour tortillas, best method is to wrap them in a damp cloth and reheat in the oven or microwave.

HIGH NOON CHILI ALE SLAW

PREP TIME: 20 minutes
REST TIME: 1 hour
6-8 SERVINGS

1	head green cabbage		1	tablespoon salt
1	medium red onion		1	tablespoon black pepper
1	poblano chili (you can substitute a jalapeño if you like it spicier, or an anaheim chili if you prefer it milder)		1	lime, juiced
			4	fluid ounces Freedom's Edge Brewing High noon Chili Ale
2	green apples			
1	handful cilantro		1	teaspoon white vinegar

1 Peel, core and julienne the green apples and cabbage.

2 Julienne the red onion and poblano pepper.

3 Dice the cilantro very fine.

4 Combine all remaining ingredients with the processed veggies. Hand mix the slaw to provide a balanced blend.

CHEF'S NOTE: The longer the slaw sits after preparation the better it will taste, at least one hour but up to 24 hours.

BREWER'S PAIRING: Freedom's Edge Brewing 1890 IPA
The slight bitterness and malty balance of the 1890 IPA lends to the salted and spicy accents of the braised pork, the citrus notes of the IPA combined with the chili ale slaw keeps your taste buds begging for more!

"VERN'S IS THE HAPPIEST PLACE IN THE WORLD! WE HAVE GREAT TOFFEE, POSITIVE PEOPLE, AND STRIVE TO MAKE PERFECT CANDY THROUGH THE PROCESS."

- PATRICK O'NEILL

JAVA JOLT TOFFEE BROWNIES

COLLABORATION	**FREEDOM'S EDGE BREWING COMPANY** Brewers, Adam Niebling & Shane Carson
	VERN'S TOFFEE HOUSE Toffee Makers, Stefanie, Patrick and Katie O'Neill

PREP TIME: 25 minutes
20 BROWNIES

½	cup Freedom's Edge Java Jolt		1	teaspoon vanilla extract
12	ounces semi-sweet chocolate chips		1-2	cups Vern's Toffee toppings (+1 cup optional for topping brownies just before they come out of the oven)
1	cup unsalted butter at room temperature		¾	cup all-purpose flour
1½	cups sugar		1	teaspoon salt
3	eggs			

1 Preheat oven to 350°.

2 Line a 9" x 13" baking dish with parchment paper.

3 In a small saucepan boil Freedom's Edge Java Jolt for about five to 10 minutes, reducing it to ¼ cup. Once reduced, allow to cool in refrigerator.

4 While Java Jolt is boiling, set a medium bowl over a saucepan of hot (but not yet simmering) water to create a double boiler. Add chocolate chips and butter to the bowl, frequently tamping (see Chef's Note) with a handheld whisk until melted and combined.

5 In a large mixing bowl beat sugar, eggs and vanilla on low speed. When thoroughly combined, slowly add melted chocolate/butter mixture, Java Jolt reduction and Vern's Toffee toppings.

6 Sift flour and salt together; fold into above mixture and immediately pour batter into lined pan.

7 Bake on oven's center rack for approximately 40 minutes. Brownies are done when toothpick comes out clean. To make these brownies really outrageous, you can sprinkle an additional cup of Vern's Toffee toppings over the top of your brownies about three minutes before they are ready to come out of the oven.

8 Remove pan from oven and allow to cool. Enjoy plain or with Vanilla Porter Caramel Sauce.

CHEF'S NOTE: Tamping is simply pushing down gently on the chocolate (and butter) repeatedly with your whisk. Chocolate should be tamped, not stirred, to prevent separation.

VANILLA PORTER CARAMEL SAUCE

COLLABORATION | **FREEDOM'S EDGE BREWING COMPANY** Brewers, Adam Niebling & Shane Carson
VERN'S TOFFEE HOUSE Toffee Makers, Stefanie, Patrick and Katie O'Neill

PREP TIME: 25 minutes
1 1/2 CUPS (ENOUGH FOR 20 BROWNIES)

12	ounces Freedom's Edge Vanilla Porter		1	cup heavy whipping cream
2	tablespoons salted butter		1	teaspoon vanilla extract
1½	cups dark brown sugar, packed		⅛	teaspoon salt

1 In a medium saucepan over medium heat, simmer Vanilla Porter for 10 minutes, stirring occasionally.

2 Stir butter and brown sugar into simmering Vanilla Porter. Cook for approximately 10 more minutes without stirring until candy thermometer reaches 232-235°. Watch carefully for the last two or three minutes to prevent burning.

3 As candy thermometer reaches 232-235°, remove saucepan from heat. Very slowly stir in the heavy whipping cream, vanilla and salt being careful to avoid any splattering. Because the heavy cream is colder than your sauce it will rapidly bubble and possibly spatter, so it is essential to add your cream slowly.

4 Briefly return saucepan to low heat and simmer, stirring constantly, for an additional three to five minutes until sauce is thickened and creamy.

5 Remove from heat completely and allow sauce to cool to room temperature (or just a little warmer). You can serve this warm over Java Jolt Toffee Brownies or chill in refrigerator to drizzle over pie or ice cream.

CHEF'S NOTE: This sauce is also delicious drizzled over bread pudding, baked apples, or vanilla ice cream that has been sprinkled with Vern's Toffee Toppings.

BREWER'S PAIRING: Combination of Freedom's Edge Vanilla Porter & Java Jolt Coffee Amber Ale
The combination of the Vanilla Porter and the Java Jolt Coffee Amber Ale Paired with the decadent chocolate brownie gives a pleasant blend of a roasty coffee presence and a rich sweetness.

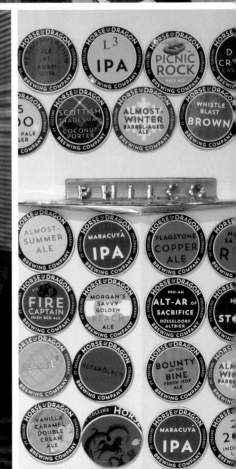

HORSE & DRAGON BREWING COMPANY

established 2014

Linsey Cornish HORSE & DRAGON BREWING COMPANY

Dave Richter THE COLORADO ROOM

Garrett Adler BLUE AGAVE GRILL

HORSE & DRAGON BREWING
COMPANY COLLABORATIONS

LINSEY CORNISH, HORSE & DRAGON BREWING COMPANY

Linsey is a well-respected and adored member of the brewery community. After studying Zoology at CSU to become an animal behaviorist, Linsey fell in love with beer and decided to pursue brewing instead. Her path as a brewer began at Odell, where she remained for four years until transitioning as a head brewer at Horse & Dragon Brewery. "It's a perfect fit. I love the owners, Carol and Tim, and the rest of the team—we are a nice little family." Linsey enjoys working alongside Carol and Tim and being immersed into the beer community. "The community of the craft beer industry is what really makes a brewer's life—it's what brought me to brewing. There is a very unique group of people who are all working towards the same goal of making phenomenal beer and having fun. We are very good at helping and supporting each other, as well as truly enjoying each other's company." Linsey's contribution to the community is her quality beers and creativity. She particularly loves to experiment and expand the palettes of beer drinkers through the ingredients she uses in her creations. While Linsey is open to making as many styles of beer as possible, she tends to produce a lot of sour beers, IPAs, and stouts. A beer that she is currently most proud of is her delicious vanilla coffee stout, Sad Panda. "I am a coffee drinker and wanted to produce a stout that could showcase beer and coffee in a way I enjoyed. I have been working on this beer for many years and am quite happy with the flavor profile it has after so many iterations. Who doesn't like to say and picture a "sad panda" while happily enjoying a delicious beer? "Despite becoming a brewer, she still loves her furry friends. "I want to adopt all of the naughty, nervous, or weird dogs."

GARRETT ADLER, BLUE AGAVE GRILL

The ambitious and talented chef Garrett is a man of many dreams with hopes to achieve them soon. "I'm 26, love what I do, and am striving to be one of the best chefs in America. I dream of the day I can be a part of a show on the Food Network." To tackle these aspirations, Garrett stands out as a chef with his vibrant personality and zesty recipe concoctions. His current culinary contribution is bringing a classy contemporary southwestern taste with a splash of Asian fusion to Blue Agave. He has developed most of the menu items with Trevor Shultz and is notorious for creating unique recipes. The Horse & Dragon beer infused guacamole is a little taste of his distinctive dishes. He particularly appreciates developing exclusive holiday specials. Inspired by his momma and Bobby Flay (the king of southwest), Garrett created a lemon lobster butter-seared scallop with avocado champagne emulsion for Mother's Day. With these delicious recipes in mind, he likes to make others' day through his creations. "Watching somebody's worries disappear after eating my food is my favorite part of being a chef." When Garrett is not in the kitchen, he can be found on the golf course, having a few beers with friends, or meeting new ones.

DAVE RICTHER, THE COLORADO ROOM

Dave's journey as a chef began with a music tour where he ate his way around the country. After acquiring a management position for his friend's rock band, Kinetix, he toured all 50 states within seven years. During this time, Dave developed a great interest for sampling various types of cuisine. "I would try as many types of food as I could. I particularly loved trying BBQ and tasting the unique flavors of each state, especially Texas and North Carolina." Once the tour came to an end, he moved back to his home state, Colorado. With his culinary adventures in mind, Dave decided to pursue cooking and received a culinary certificate at Cook Street in Denver. He later reconnected with his two college dorm mates, Justin and Danny, who were looking to start a restaurant called The Colorado Room. Dave decided to join them and became the head chef. He designed the full menu and was inspired by the countless slider sandwiches he made for his friends at football parties he hosted. "We focus on unique slider sandwiches, wings, and poutine. One of my favorites is the Bison Sandwich, complete with slow roasted bison brisket, pickled cucumber, carrots, teriyaki sauce, chilies, and topped with fresh cilantro." When Dave is not creating insanely tasty sandwiches, he still enjoys the occasional live music concert.

"I LOVE THE OWNERS,
CAROL AND TIM, AND THE
REST OF THE TEAM—WE
ARE A NICE LITTLE FAMILY."

- LINSEY CORNISH

AGITATED AARDVARK ALE INFUSED GUACAMOLE

COLLABORATION | **HORSE & DRAGON BREWING COMPANY** Brewer, Linsey Cornish
BLUE AGAVE GRILL Chef, Garrett Adler

PREP TIME: 20 Minutes
6 SERVINGS

6	tomatillos, halved		½	teaspoon garlic powder
1	cup Horse & Dragon Agitated Aardvark Ale		¼	teaspoon coriander
1	cup water		½	lime, juiced
3	avocados, smashed		2	tablespoons Horse & Dragon Agitated Aardvark Ale
3	tablespoons cilantro, chopped			
3	tablespoons roma tomatoes, diced			
½	teaspoon salt			

Combine tomatillos, Horse & Dragon Aardvark Ale, and water in medium sauté pan, and bring to a boil. Turn to medium and simmer for about 20 minutes, or until tomatillos are soft. Put in blender and blend until you have a nice purée. Cool in fridge. Combine purée with remaining ingredients.

CHEF'S NOTE: Add all of your ingredients together except for the beer/tomatillo purée. After you have mixed everything, add your purée a little at a time until you have your perfect consistency.

BREWER'S PAIRING: Horse & Dragon Almost Summer Ale

I would recommend pairing the Agitated Aardvark Guacamole with a flavorful blonde or summer ale. Horse & Dragon's Almost Summer Ale is a perfect match for this dish. The depth of citrusy and malt flavors stands up to the richness and complexity of the guacamole.

"WATCHING SOMEBODY'S WORRIES DISAPPEAR AFTER EATING MY FOOD IS MY FAVORITE PART OF BEING A CHEF."

- GARRETT ADLER

ALMOST SUMMER ALE PINEAPPLE CEVICHE & CILANTRO MINT PESTO

COLLABORATION	**HORSE & DRAGON BREWING COMPANY** Brewer, Linsey Cornish **BLUE AGAVE GRILL** Chef, Garrett Adler

ALMOST SUMMER PINEAPPLE CEVICE

PREP TIME: 9 hours
4 SERVINGS

6	ounces sea scallops, diced	1½	tablespoons mint, chopped
6	limes, juiced	1½	tablespoons cilantro, chopped
3	tablespoons white onion, diced		jalapeño, diced
3	tablespoons roma tomatoes, diced		salt to taste
½	cup Horse & Dragon Almost Summer Ale	½	teaspoon white pepper
3	tablespoons pineapple, diced	1	cucumber

1 Combine sea scallops, white onion and tomatoes. Cover with lime juice. Store in refrigerator for at least eight hours.

2 After eight hours, drain lime juice from scallops. Then combine with remaining ingredients including the beer.

3 To make cucumber cups, take one cucumber and peel. Then cut into 1½ inch cups, discard most of the seeds leaving a little at the bottom. Fill your cups with the ceviche and serve.

CILANTRO MINT PESTO

PREP TIME: 7 minutes
4 SERVINGS

1	bundle cilantro	2	tablespoons parmesan cheese
2	ounces mint	1½	tablespoons chopped garlic
3	tablespoons olive oil		salt to taste

In food processor or blender, combine all ingredients except oil and purée. Slowly add oil until all is combined.

CHEF'S NOTE: You don't have to use pineapple for this—it's great with watermelon, peach, mango and papaya as well.

BREWER'S PAIRING: Horse & Dragon's Picnic Rock Pale Ale
This Ceviche has some wonderful beer pairing notes, especially since it is so well balanced between spicy, and tropical fruity. It would pair beautifully with a pale ale, like Horse & Dragon's Picnic Rock Pale Ale. This beer's tropical fruit notes will complement the pineapple, or any other tropical fruit you choose to use. The hop character of the beer will also enhance the jalapeno's spiciness, and finally the fresh earthy character of the cucumber will balance out all the fruit and hop characters of the beer leaving a very satisfying cooling sensation.

CHOCOLATE MINT STOUT PORK LOIN MOLE

ABORATION | **HORSE & DRAGON BREWING COMPANY** Brewer, Linsey Cornish
BLUE AGAVE GRILL Chef, Garrett Adler

PREP TIME: 1 hour
4 SERVINGS
4-6 OUNCE PORK LOIN

SPICES FOR PORK RUB

2	tablespoons salt
1	tablespoon cumin
¼	teaspoon clove
1	teaspoon black pepper
1	teaspoon oregano
1½	teaspoons chili powder
1	teaspoon cinnamon
1	tablespoon paprika

MOLE SAUCE INGREDIENTS

¼	cup canola oil
6	yellow corn tortillas, toasted
1	can chipotles in adobo
½	red onion
6	cloves chopped garlic
¾	cup sliced almonds
2	tablespoons chicken base
3	cups water
2	cups Horse & Dragon Mint Chocolate Stout
6	roma tomatoes, diced
¼	teaspoon cinnamon
⅓	cup dried cherries
1½	tablespoons agave nectar, or honey
½	lime, juiced

Combine all spices and coat pork loin. Set aside.

In a medium sauté pan over high heat, add half your oil and toast almonds, then set aside. Add remaining oil to a medium sauté pan, and over high heat combine your red onion, chopped garlic, and chipotles. Boil for about two minutes. In a food processor or blender combine toasted almonds, your boiled chipotle mixture, toasted corn tortillas, and 1½ cups of chicken broth (combine the chicken base with water to make broth). Blend until smooth.

Now in large sauté pan, combine remaining ingredients and boil for about 10 minutes. Remove from heat and add to the blender full of ingredients. Blend until smooth, strain, and hold hot.

In a large sauté pan, heat up one cup of oil and brown the pork loin. Finish the loin in the oven; be sure to cook internal temperature to 145°.

JALAPEÑO SWEET POTATO CAKE

COLLABORATION	**HORSE & DRAGON BREWING COMPANY**
	Brewer, Linsey Cornish
	BLUE AGAVE GRILL Chef, Garrett Adler

PREP TIME: 25 minutes
4 SERVINGS

1	sweet potato
4	ounces goat cheese
½	jalapeño, diced
2	teaspoons brown sugar
1	teaspoon salt
1	cup flour
2	eggs, beaten
2	cups all-purpose breadcrumbs
2	cups canola oil

Boil potato until soft, then smash. Combine all remaining ingredients and cool. Once cool, form four patties, then dip in flour. Add beaten egg, and then bread crumbs. In a medium sauté pan, heat oil and fry each side until golden brown.

CHEF'S NOTE: When serving, I recommend letting the pork rest for a few minutes, and cutting the pork into ¼ inch slices. Serve on top of the sweet potato cake.

BREWER'S PAIRING: Horse & Dragon's Total Ale ESB Due to the complexity of the mole, I recommend pairing it with a beer that will complement but not overpower the dish and allow all of the nuances of the ingredients to shine. Styles such as Brown Ales, Dunkel Lagers, and ESBs (Extra Special Bitters) would be a perfect fit. Horse & Dragon's Total Ale ESB is a great match for this dish with its clean and delicate hop finish and malty backbone. The beer will support the richness of the mole as well as cut the subtle spiciness.

3 MEAT, 3 BEAN FIREMAN RED CHILI

| COLLABORATION | **HORSE & DRAGON BREWING COMPANY** Brewer, Linsey Cornish |
| | **THE COLORADO ROOM** Chef, Dave Richter |

PREP TIME: 30 minutes
COOK TIME: 4 hours
10 SERVINGS

4	cups yellow onion, diced	2	cans (30 ounce) black beans
2	cups green chiles, diced	2	cans (30 ounce) red kidney beans
1	cup jalapeño, diced	2	cans (30 ounce) pinto beans
2	cups red bell pepper, diced	1	can (30 ounce) petite diced tomato
1	pound ground beef	6	ounces tomato paste
1	pound ground pork	8	tablespoons chili powder
1	pound rib eye steak		salt and pepper
4	cups Horse & Dragon Fireman Red	5	tablespoons cumin
5	cloves garlic, minced		

1 Prep the first four ingredients.

2 Brown the meats in a pot, one at a time, removing the meat once browned and leaving the fat in the pot.

3 After all meat has been cooked, add the diced veggies and sauté until the onions are translucent.

4 Add all the beer at once, bring to a boil, and simmer until the liquid has reduced in half (10 minutes).

5 Once reduced, add the remaining ingredients, stirring to ensure they are incorporated.

6 Slowly bring to a simmer, stirring frequently to prevent sticking to the bottom and burning. Simmer for three hours, until the chili has thickened.

7 Serve hot!

CHEF'S NOTE: It is important to keep the chili at a very low temperature and to stir frequently to prevent burning. Recipe can also be made vegetarian, or with different types of ground meat. If you would like, serve with shredded cheddar cheese, sour cream and thinly sliced scallions!

BREWER'S PAIRING: Horse & Dragon Stout or NoCo IPA

I am always torn between stouts and hoppy beers when it comes to pairing with chili. The roasted malt and chocolaty flavors of a stout complement the bean and meat ingredients, and the creamy finish will soothe the chili's heat. Horse & Dragon's Stout does this extremely well. On the other hand, hoppy beers lend themselves well to spicy food, actually enhancing the spiciness. Horse & Dragon's NoCo IPA is a great pairing with this chili for many reasons. Its fruity hop aroma will complement the tomato character of the chili and the malty toffee notes will play well with the meat flavors, finishing with a hoppy bitterness that will cut the chili's richness.

BEER BRAISED LAMB SHOULDER

COLLABORATION	HORSE & DRAGON BREWING COMPANY Brewer, Linsey Cornish
	THE COLORADO ROOM Chef, Dave Richter

PREP TIME: 30 minutes
COOK TIME: 7 hours
12-16 SERVINGS

3-5	pounds lamb shoulder		4	oz thyme
8	cups Horse & Dragon Sad Panda Stout		4	oz pound parsley
3	carrots		4	bay leaves
1	large onion		5	cloves garlic
1	bunch celery		4	cups chicken stock

1 Preheat oven to 250°.

2 Season the lamb with salt and pepper.

3 Heat a large roasting pan on high and sear all sides of the lamb shoulder. Once all sides have a slight crust on them, remove the meat and hold for later.

4 Add the onions, celery and carrots (all rough chopped into smaller similar sized pieces), and begin to brown.

5 Once browned add all the beer at once and bring to a boil. Reduce the beer in half.

6 Add the chicken stock and remaining ingredients and bring back to a boil.

7 Add the lamb back into the liquid, cover with aluminum foil and bake in oven for seven hours or until the lamb shreds when touched.

8 Remove from oven and take lamb out of liquid to cool. Once cooled shred the lamb.

CHEF'S NOTE: Serve as a sandwich with a mint pesto, beer mustard, melted gouda cheese, roasted red peppers and shoestring potatoes. This recipe can also be done with lamb shanks, and then presented as full bone in shanks. Serve with potato and fava beans, drizzle with the braising liquid.

BREWER'S PAIRING: Horse & Dragon Whistle Blast Honey Brown Ale

The nutty, toffee and caramel characters present in brown ales make them perfect for pairing with darker cooked meats. Horse & Dragon's Whistle Blast Honey Brown Ale is a great example with this dish. It has a smooth toffee sweetness that will pair well with the braised lamb and complement the earthiness of the browned veggies. The stout addition to the dish will really bring out the subtle chocolate and roast characters in the beer as well.

SNOWBANK BREWING COMPANY

established 2014

Dave Rosso SNOWBANK BREWING COMPANY

Sacha Steinhauser TASTY HARMONY

Sara Gilman UMAMI MOBILE EATERY

Toby and Alix Gadd NUANCE CHOCOLATE

SNOWBANK BREWING COMPANY COLLABORATIONS

TASTY HARMONY
UMAMI MOBILE EATERY *and*
NUANCE CHOCOLATE

DAVE ROSSO, SNOWBANK BREWING COMPANY

Dave Rosso, owner and brewer at Snowbank Brewing Company, pushes the limits of innovative and traditional beers. As Dave sips on his Coffee Pale Ale and pets his furry companion, Simcoe (named after hops), he explains how he doesn't specialize in a certain style of beer. "We use modern innovation and techniques not allowed by typical German brewing laws. We make the best beers we can and incorporate community by cultivating collaborations." Dave's newest invention is his S'more Stout, infused with local cocoa nibs from Nuance Chocolate, graham crackers, vanilla, and topped with marshmallows from Stuff'n Mallows (roasted at the brewery). Aside from brewing unique and collaborative beers, Dave incorporates an atmosphere into his brewery that is inspired by Colorado. "When I moved from Nebraska to Colorado in my 20s, I fell in love with the state. As a result, Snowbank is all about the Colorado lifestyle." The cozy taproom is filled with beautiful photos of the Rockies by local artists and the signature brewery snowflake logos. Many of his beer names have Colorado themes such as Colorado Red or Bike Trail Pale. Dave is a man of many talents as he balances his career as an electrical engineer and a brewer. "I like the technical challenge of engineering which translates well into brewing. Since I spent a lot of my free time home brewing, I decided to make it part of my career." Dave also enjoys backpacking in the mountains and running.

SACHA STEINHAUSER, TASTY HARMONY

In 2009 Sacha and his wife Jill opened a Fort Collins staple, Tasty Harmony. Sacha offers organic plant based vegan fare to the community with hopes to reach more people with the message of plants. "My approach to vegan cuisine is seeing it not as a way of life, but as a genre of cooking, one that doesn't get a lot of credit when compared to more mainstream types of food." Sacha designs creative dishes with raw ingredients that are mostly made in house such as his cache cheese and seitan. "My job is to create meals that are fun to play with, and delicious." He will sometimes incorporate his discoveries from traveling throughout Asia into his dishes. For example, one of his most popular plates is his delectable BBQ Pulled Jackfruit, which is a 6-hour cooking process complete with jackfruit, house made BBQ sauce, coleslaw, tomatoes, red onion, and pickles. Most of the produce used in these tasty meals is home grown by his wife Jill. Another way Sacha introduces his customers to the significance of plants is through his medicinal drink selection. "It's a great way to incorporate medicinal value into your happy hour," laughs Sacha. Behind the bar, Sacha has a drip system that grows all of the fresh herbs used in the drinks. There are a variety of cocktails to choose from such as "the drink that makes it impossible for me to have bad thoughts," which is a bright and effervescent cocktail with lemon grass, combucha, fresh tulsi, jalapeño, blue agave, and lime. Aside from introducing the community to the adventurous world of plant foods, Sacha is busy raising five children and exploring the Colorado Rockies as much as he can.

SNOWBANK BREWING COLLABORATIONS

SARA GILMAN, UMAMI MOBILE EATERY

Chef Sara Gilman's interest in cooking developed as a child when she acted as her mother's little helper in the kitchen. "We created cookbooks from scratch for school. I was always intrigued by the process of combining ingredients to create delicious meals." As Sara grew older, she was influenced by her close friends and family to develop her knowledge as a chef. "I often apply cooking tips from others and challenge myself to create new flavors. I never follow recipes. I've learned from trial and error and use ingredients as my form of inspiration." Eager to jump into the world of "civilization," Sara moved from a small town in Lander, Wyoming to the vibrant city of Fort Collins. What soon unfolded for her was an unexpected mobile foodie adventure. After her move, Sara became acquainted with Chuck and Tami Tallent, owner of an Asian fusion food truck, Umami Mobile Eatery. She began to work with them and eventually assumed full ownership. "I like to try cooking something different. Before Umami, experimenting with Asian dishes was a new challenge for me—so I said let's play! I'm actively pursuing my passion one dish at a time, sharing that special moment of the customer's first bite." Sara enjoys developing Asian fusion creations that are vegan, vegetarian, and gluten free. She explains, "I have fun playing with flavors that you don't usually expect such as Thai nachos covered with peanut sauce, cilantro, and cheese." When she isn't cooking, Sara often hangs out with her adored pups, Winston and Larka.

TOBY GADD, NUANCE CHOCOLATE

If your heart is made of chocolate, visiting chocolate maker and owner, Toby Gadd at Nuance Chocolate will be your next loyal sweet spot. When you step into his shop, it is hard not to smile when taking in the delightful chocolate aromas and sampling his one-of-a-kind handmade chocolates. This is not your typical chocolatier—it is better. Nuance Chocolate is a true bean-to-bar chocolate shop that produces small batch chocolates locally at a factory in Fort Collins. Toby receives his ethically sourced cacao beans from 17 plus regions around the globe and currently holds the record for the widest range of single origin chocolates in the world. He offers an assortment of chocolate bars, truffles, sipping hot chocolate, and more. There are around 30 different varieties of chocolate bars and more than 22 truffle flavors. "We offer the most unusual truffles out there. I'm not sure anyone else has put hops and dark chocolate malt in a truffle before. It's amazing!" His truffles range from classic to innovative such as his Rose Water and Champagne to the Snake Bite (complete with hints of tequila, sea salt, lime, and chili). Toby is an acclaimed chocoholic. "I've always loved chocolate, who doesn't? If I meet someone that doesn't like chocolate, I don't know if I can trust them." When Toby isn't making chocolate, you may find him sneaking a few pieces of chocolate while he is competing in the Ultra Endurance Mountain Bike competition from Denver to Durango.

WHEAT BERRY AND SMOKED RED KURI SQUASH SALAD
WITH SNOW BANK WHEAT BEER VINAIGRETTE

COLLABORATION | **SNOWBANK BREWING COMPANY** Brewer, Dave Rosso
| **TASTY HARMONY** Chef, Sacha Steinhauser

PREP TIME: 1 hour prep time
4 SERVINGS

2	cups red winter wheat berries		½	cup olive oil
3	cups water		1	cup Snowbank Moon Arête Wheat
1	teaspoon salt		2	teaspoons salt
1	head lacinato kale, chopped		1	teaspoon black pepper
2	pounds red kuri squash		1	tablespoon dried tarragon
2	tablespoons pine nuts		⅓	cup honey
½	cup shallots, chopped		¼	cup apple cider vinegar
2	teaspoons garlic, chopped			

1 Combine wheat berries, water and salt in a medium saucepan and simmer for an hour, or until wheat berries are tender but slightly chewy. When done, take off heat and add kale to hot water for one minute to soften the dark greens. Drain water thoroughly and set aside.

2 Cut squash in half and deseed. Continue to cut the squash into wedges like a cantaloupe. Place wood chips in stovetop smoker according to manufacturer's directions and put squash in smoker. Place on stove at medium to low and turn on ventilation fan in kitchen. Smoke for 25 minutes or until squash is tender but not mushy. Take off heat and cool. Cut squash, cut off the skin, chop squash into larger pieces and add to wheat berries and kale.

3 Sauté shallots in olive oil until translucent, add garlic, and sauté for another minute. Add beer, salt, pepper, tarragon, honey and apple cider vinegar. Reduce vinaigrette for 20 minutes on medium low and then take off heat to cool to room temperature or slightly warmer. Toss into the salad and serve at room temperature.

CHEF'S NOTE: This is a hearty salad that is great on colder days. Obviously there is a wheat theme going on with this one, and with all the bad wrap that wheat gets these days, I'm still a believer and I think this pairing will prove it. Although the recipe calls for a stovetop smoker, it is not the end of the world to just bake the squash. However, I highly recommend investing in one (they're only like 20 bucks) to infuse a great flavor to heartier dishes.

BREWER'S PAIRING: Snowbank Moon Arête
The smokiness of the squash and chewy wheat berries marry with the subtle undertones of wheat and hint of banana of the Moon Arête Wheat while accentuating the freshness of the crisp kale.

SEITAN SCHNITZEL
WITH SNOW BANK RED ALE MUSHROOM GRAVY, MASHERS, AND GARLICKY GREENS

COLLABORATION	SNOWBANK BREWING COMPANY Brewer, Dave Rosso
	TASTY HARMONY Chef, Sacha Steinhauser

PREP TIME: 45 minutes
6 SERVINGS

SEITAN SCHNITZEL
2	packages of your favorite seitan

BATTER
1	cup unbleached white flour
1	tablespoon nutritional yeast
¾	teaspoon salt
½	teaspoon black pepper
1	cup unsweetened soy milk
¼	cup water

DREDGE
2	cups unbleached white flour
2	cups bread crumbs
	extra oil and flour for frying
5	large Russet or Idaho potatoes
½	cup Earth Balance
½	cup unsweetened soy milk
	salt and pepper
1	head rainbow chard, roughly chopped
2	teaspoons garlic

GRAVY
2	portobello caps, roughly chopped
½	cup yellow onion, finely chopped
1½	teaspoon garlic, chopped
⅓	cup organic canola oil
½	cup whole wheat flour
½	cup nutritional yeast
2½	cups water
1	cup Snowbank Colorado Red Ale
¼	cup tamari
½	teaspoon salt
½	teaspoon black pepper
1	teaspoon ground sage
1	teaspoon ground thyme

BATTER

Mix all the batter ingredients together with a whisk until smooth. Mix dredge ingredients together. Set aside.

GRAVY

Toast the whole wheat flour and nutritional yeast in a fry pan until fragrant, careful not to burn. Sauté onion and mushrooms in the canola oil until most of the liquid from the mushrooms has evaporated. Add garlic and sauté for another minute. Add the flour mix and stir into the oil until all the flour has been absorbed into the oil. Add in the liquids while whisking vigorously until all the liquid has been absorbed by the flour. Add everything else and simmer for 15 minutes while stirring every couple of minutes to prevent burning.

MASHERS

Cut up potatoes and boil until soft. Drain and mash with Earth Balance, unsweetened soymilk, salt and pepper.

GREENS

In sauté pan, heat a tablespoon of oil and add chopped garlic. Immediately add chard and sauté on low until wilted. Add salt and pepper to taste

SCHNITZEL

Cut seitan into thin but wide pieces if possible. Coat in plain flour, dip into batter, and then cover in dredge. Let rest for several minutes before pan frying. In shallow pan, put about ¼ inch of oil and bring to heat. Test a piece first to make sure it's not too hot or cold. Add schnitzel pieces and fry until golden brown, turning over halfway.

CHEF'S NOTE: Growing up with a Czech dad, I ate lots of schnitzel. I chose this recipe to pair with the red ale because 1) people tend to not think of vegan food as meaty and satiating and 2) the red ale is so delicious it needs something as equally delicious! Seitan is an old Chinese invention that is a meat-like texture but made from wheat gluten. Sometimes it is referred to as wheat meat. Pick your seitan wisely or make your own. It's fun and easy to make, however if you do buy some from the store, make sure it's salty enough. There's nothing worse than chewing on bland wheat gluten.

BREWER'S PAIRING: Snowbank Colorado Red Ale
The citrus hop character and moderate bitterness of the Colorado Red Ale balance with the rich and robust flavors of this dish.

TASTY VEGAN MOCHA COOKIES

COLLABORATION | **SNOWBANK BREWING COMPANY** Brewer, Dave Rosso
TASTY HARMONY Chef, Sacha Steinhauser

PREP TIME: 20 minutes
YIELDS 6 LARGE COOKIES

COOKIE DOUGH

1	cup barley flour
¼	cup Dutch cocoa powder
¾	teaspoon baking soda
½	teaspoon salt
3	teaspoons Ener-G Egg Replacer
4	tablespoons warm water
1	cup organic sugar
⅓	cup organic canola oil + 1 tablespoon
1	teaspoon vanilla extract
¼	cup porter
1½	cup rolled oats

GLAZE

1	cup Snowbank Pawnee Porter
1	double shot espresso
3	cups semi-sweet chocolate chips

COOKIES

Preheat oven to 350°. Mix all the dry stuff together. In small bowl, whisk the Ener-G Egg Replacer with warm water until foamy. In separate bowl, mix the oil and sugar together until creamy, and then add egg replacer, porter and vanilla. Mix well, then add to dry ingredients. When the dry and wet ingredients are mixed, fold in oats. Scoop into balls (do not flatten) and put on parchment lined cookie sheet. Bake for 11 minutes.

GLAZE

Simmer espresso and porter over low heat for 15 minutes to reduce mixture. Add chocolate chips and stir until chocolate has melted and glaze is smooth. Take off heat, let cool for several minutes to thicken, then dunk cookies into mixture or drizzle on top of cookies.

CHEF'S NOTE: This cookie was a no brainer to pair with the porter. We have a cake at the restaurant that we make with whatever porter or stout we have on tap but I wanted to make an easy hand held sweet you can eat on the go. With the porter in the dough and glaze, you get a double whammy of dark goodness in every bite.

BREWER'S PAIRING: Snowbank Inclination IPA
The resiny hop bitterness of the Inclination IPA accentuates the earthiness of the rolled oats while contrasting the sweetness of the rich mocha flavor.

"I NEVER FOLLOW RECIPES. I'VE LEARNED FROM TRIAL AND ERROR AND USE INGREDIENTS AS MY FORM OF INSPIRATION."

- SARA GILMAN

SILENT SNOW WHITE IPA INFUSED HUMMUS

COLLABORATION | **SNOWBANK BREWING COMPANY** Brewer, Dave Rosso
UMAMI MOBILE EATERY Chef, Sara Gilman

PREP TIME: 5 minutes
3-4 SERVINGS

2	cans chickpeas		1	tablespoon red pepper flakes
1	cup Snowbank Silent Snow White IPA		2	tablespoons minced shallot
¼	cup parmesan cheese		3	tablespoons minced garlic
1-2	tablespoons fresh lemon juice		2	tablespoons tahini
1	teaspoon salt		¼-½	cup extra virgin olive oil

Combine all ingredients in a food processor except for the olive oil. Blend until the hummus is coarsely puréed. Once the hummus is coarsely puréed slowly add the olive oil with the food processor running; this is a key step to a smooth textured hummus. After reaching desired consistency, taste for seasoning. Serve chilled or at room temperature with your favorite dipping companions!

CHEF'S NOTE: The parmesan cheese is not a deal breaker in this recipe. It acts as a flavor enhancer but can be left out as needed.

BREWER'S PAIRING: Snowbank Silent Snow IPA
The Silent Snow IPA pairs well with the infused hummus because the jasmine and orange blossom tones from the beer enhance the citrus flavors from the fresh lemon juice.

COLORADO RED INFUSED SOY GINGER GLAZED SALMON

COLLABORATION | **SNOWBANK BREWING COMPANY** Brewer, Dave Rosso
UMAMI MOBILE EATERY Chef, Sara Gilman

PREP TIME: 15 minutes
COOKING TIME: 15 minutes
2-3 SERVINGS

1	cup Snowbank Colorado Red Ale		2	teaspoons shredded ginger
½	cup soy sauce		1	teaspoon sesame oil
⅛	cup red wine vinegar		2	tablespoons brown sugar
⅛	cup rice wine vinegar		1	tablespoon sesame seeds
2	teaspoons minced garlic			corn starch slurry
			2-3	salmon fillets

In a saucepan, combine the red ale, soy sauce, vinegars, garlic, ginger, sesame oil and sesame seeds. Turn on medium heat and let come to a light boil. Reduce the red ale down. On the side, make a corn starch slurry by combining about ½ cup corn starch and some water. Start by adding about a ½ cup of water and stir until combined. Add more water as needed to get to a syrup-like consistency. When adding the slurry to the mixture, the sauce should be hot and boiling. Have a whisk handy to help incorporate the slurry into the sauce. The sauce will thicken quickly after this step. Turn off the heat and add the brown sugar. Whisk until combined. Taste the sauce for seasoning.

Prepare the salmon fillets by adding salt and pepper to both sides. Add a little squirt of lemon to both sides of the fillet for added flavor. Heat a sauté pan over medium heat. Add one to two tablespoons olive oil or coconut oil. Sear the salmon fillets on each side for approximately two minutes. Finish the salmon in an oven at 350° for four to eight minutes for desired doneness.

Serve over a bed of rice with some tasty veggies and glaze the salmon fillets.

CHEF'S NOTE: The consistency of this sauce is completely subjective. For a thicker sauce make a thicker slurry and vice versa.

BREWER'S PAIRING: Snowbank Colorado Red Ale
The peach and ribbon candy fruit notes from the Colorado Red Ale contrast with the soy ginger salty spice to create a nice harmony.

KANOM KROK
(COCONUT CAKES WITH PAWNEE PORTER)

COLLABORATION	**SNOWBANK BREWING COMPANY** Brewer, Dave Rosso
	UMAMI MOBILE EATERY Chef, Sara Gilman

PREP TIME: 15 minutes
COOKING TIME: 30 minutes
5-6 SERVINGS

3	cans coconut milk
1	cup Snowbank Pawnee Porter
¼	cup sugar + 1 tablespoon sugar
2½	cups tapioca flour
3	tablespoons uncooked white rice

⅓	cup freshly shredded coconut
3	cups rice flour
2	teaspoons sea salt
2-3	tablespoons peanut or coconut oil
	green onion (optional)
	cilantro (optional)

Spoon out the creamiest part of the coconut milk and put aside the rest. You want 1¾ cups of the creamy coconut milk for the topping and the rest for the batter. In a saucepan, put the creamy coconut milk, ½ cup porter and ¼ cup sugar. Heat just enough to break up clumps. Allow to cool and add tapioca flour. For a thicker sauce, add more tapioca flour. Set aside for later.

Using a bowl, whisk out any clumps from remaining coconut milk. Using a clean coffee grinder, grind the uncooked rice and add to the milk. Add the freshly shredded coconut. Mix in ½ cup porter. Add the rice flour, salt and one tablespoon sugar to the batter. Mix until well blended.

Heat a griddle on medium heat. Once heated, brush with peanut oil or coconut oil. Using a scoop, drop the batter on the griddle forming little cakes. Allow the batter to bubble and pop before flipping (three to five minutes). The finished product should resemble pancakes. Finish the cakes with the sweet coconut cream from earlier and enjoy!

CHEF'S NOTE: Traditionally, this dish should be cooked using a "kanom krok pan." From experience, using a griddle and forming small pancakes is the easier approach to this recipe.

BREWER'S PAIRING: Snowbank Moon Arête
The honey, fresh bread, and banana flavors of the Moon Arête complement the sweet coconut flavor of the pancakes.

"I'VE ALWAYS LOVED CHOCOLATE, WHO DOESN'T? IF I MEET SOMEONE THAT DOESN'T LIKE CHOCOLATE, I DON'T KNOW IF I CAN TRUST THEM."

- TOBY GADD

HIS NIBS' FAMOUS SAUERKRAUT

COLLABORATION | **SNOWBANK BREWING COMPANY** Brewer, Dave Rosso
NUANCE CHOCOLATE Chocolate Makers, Toby and Alix Gadd

PREP TIME: 10 minutes
COOK TIME: 4-8 hours
YIELDS 1/4 CUP

16	ounces sauerkraut	1	tablespoon butter
12	ounces Snowbank Pawnee Porter	1	tablespoon Nuance Chocolate Ghana Cacao Nibs
2	tablespoons sugar		

Combine all ingredients in a medium saucepan. Simmer four to eight hours, adding water as needed to keep sauerkraut from drying out.

CHEF'S NOTE: After simmering for several hours, sauerkraut's sharp bite mellows but retains its tang in this flavorful, savory side dish. Try it with sausages, pork loin, or even with your Thanksgiving turkey.

BREWER'S PAIRING: Snowbank Ghana Chocolate Stout
The Ghana Chocolate Stout is made with Nuance Ghana cacao beans and has a very rich chocolate flavor. The rich malty sweetness balances the acidity of the sauerkraut.

MOON OVER CAMERON PASS SNACK LOAF

COLLABORATION | **SNOWBANK BREWING COMPANY** Brewer, Dave Rosso
NUANCE CHOCOLATE Chocolate Makers, Toby and Alix Gadd

PREP TIME: 20 minutes
COOK TIME: 45 minutes
YIELDS 8 (3 OUNCE) SLICES

2½	cups whole wheat pastry flour or all-purpose flour		4	ounces Nuance Chocolate 70% Ghana dark chocolate, coarsely chopped
½	cup old fashioned oats		½	cup walnuts, coarsely chopped
3	tablespoons sugar		12	ounces Snowbank Moon Arête
2	teaspoons baking powder		2	tablespoons butter, melted
1	teaspoon salt			

Preheat oven to 375°. Combine flour, oats, sugar, baking powder and salt in a three-quart bowl. Stir in walnuts and chocolate. Add beer and stir until just combined. Pour into a greased 4" x 8" standard loaf pan. Bake 40 minutes. Carefully brush the top of the loaf with melted butter. Bake five to 10 minutes longer until top is golden brown and a toothpick comes out clean.

CHEF'S NOTE: This loaf is substantial and chocolatey, but not overly sweet. Try it with spreadable goat cheese and a slice of Honeycrisp apple as a perfect lunch on a mountain hike.

BREWER'S PAIRING: Snowbank Moon Arête
The Moon Arête pairs nicely with the snack loaf because it has earthy aromas with a hint of honey, and flavors of fresh bread.

ZWEI BREWING

established 2014

Kirk Lombardi ZWEI BREWING

Scott "Manno" Manning TAPS SPORTS BAR AND GRILL

Heather Beckman SILVER GRILL CAFÉ

Mike Neal MARY'S MOUNTAIN COOKIES

ZWEI BREWING COLLABORATIONS

TAPS SPORTS BAR AND GRILL
SILVER GRILL CAFÉ
and MARY'S MOUNTAIN COOKIES

KIRK LOMBARDI, ZWEI BREWING

Sitting in a quaint Biergarten under a chestnut tree while taking in a hearty stein of delicious Helles in the heart of Munich, Germany was the beginning of something beautiful for Kirk. Not only did he experience Oktoberfest and sample a variety of Germany's finest, he also embarked on 20 private tours of Bavaria's local breweries. Coupled with Kirk's positive experiences with the brewers and new infatuation for German beer, he had immediate aspirations to bring back a little taste of Germany's brews to his hometown of Fort Collins. In 2014, Kirk and his brother Eric established Zwei Brewing. "We wanted to create a warm neighborhood community gathering place, offering German specialty beers on the south end of Fort Collins." Their brewery is one where you can relive your trip to Germany or fall in love with German beers. The distinctive taproom sets the tone of an authentic German experience because of the large pint glasses, a Biergarten, and several German classics (Pils, Dunkelweizen, Helles, etc.). As Kirk puts it, "I want customers to leave with a satisfying new appreciation for German style beers, three t-shirts, a growler, and a good buzz."

SCOTT "MANNO" MANNING, TAPS SPORTS BAR AND GRILL

When you walk into Taps Sports Bar and Grill and smell the smoky bacon and beef aroma you'll wish you had a juicy hamburger in your hands. This laid back sports bar is one of the few places in town that customers are able to watch the game and grab a burger that is smoked in house. The man behind the smoker is Scott Manning, a legendary BBQ grill master. In 2012, Scott partnered with his friend Mark Spring and became the executive chef for Taps. Scott explains, "We have so much fun with the smoker—I can't get enough. I love experimenting with smoked blue cheese, almonds, salmon and pulled pork. We have some darn good BBQ!" Scott takes his smoking skills to the next level by participating in the annual The Kansas City BBQ Society competition. He is able to meet chefs from around the world and often returns home with a medal for his smoked brisket and pork. Scott's biggest critics are not the judges from the competition, but rather his beloved wife and four kids. "They love to give me feedback whether it is at home or when they come visit me at the restaurant." One of Scott's best chefs secrets is smoking with a happy heart. "Cook with joy and it will be sure to show. I enjoy sharing the love I have for food with others." When Scott isn't busy smoking up a storm, he creates ice carving sculptures and woodcarvings. His latest project is sculpting little carved wooden creatures on his property in the woods.

ZWEI BREWING COLLABORATIONS

HEATHER BECKMAN, SILVER GRILL CAFÉ

Heather's adventurous spirit led her to study under various pastry chefs and manage restaurants in both St. John and Greece. In the midst of her international work, she embarked on several culinary expeditions and traveled every six months to different countries. After a few years of taking in diverse cultural flavors, Heather moved to Fort Collins to settle down with her husband and begin a family. Her creativity further developed as she began to work at The Silver Grill Café (the oldest established restaurant in Fort Collins, built in 1912). Heather's explorative nature transitioned from traveling to cooking. "As my palate changed, I became more experimental with cooking. John (owner of Silver Grill) lets me spread my wings and try different items!" Her craving for cooking also feeds into her home life. "My family and I often experiment with various ingredients and create an extravagant meal together. Many times we come up with new menu items for Silver Grill. We have so much fun cooking as a family." Heather also enjoys collaborating with local breweries. She helped develop the Cinnsational Ale, a delicious cinnamon flavored beer, with Odell using Silver Grill's famous cinnamon rolls. Heather is also working on a beer cheese soup with Pateros Creek Brewing and continues to test out new dishes.

MIKE NEAL, MARY'S MOUNTAIN COOKIES

"I try to have a cookie a day. The times I eat a few too many cookies are when I start making cookie dough early in the morning. Once I begin eating taster bites at the beginning of the process, I'm doomed. Today however, I made 900 pounds of cookie dough and was a good boy," smiles Mike, an owner of a Fort Collins favorite, Mary's Mountain Cookies. This crafty cookie connoisseur has had an infatuation for cookies since he can remember. He is thankful to be in an industry that encompasses his love for cookies and thrives off of the joy he spreads through his establishment. "The whole cookie business is nice—It's a good gig. The employees are happy and we make people smile along the way." Mike assumed the Old Town franchise after working for several years with Mary, creator and original owner of Mary's Mountain cookies. His goal as an owner is "to create new flavors while working towards cookie domination, one delicious cookie at a time." His team often comes up with out of the ordinary flavors such as the blueberry cheesecake, or S'more cookie. After baking and tasting thousands of pounds of cookies a week, Mike remains fit. He is an avid trail runner, and often competes in ultra-marathons sometimes running over 100 miles. Mike is also known to have a mean backhand at ping-pong and occasionally loves to surf around the world and travel.

GERMAN PRETZEL STICKS & ZWEI DUNKEL BEER MUSTARD

COLLABORATION	**ZWEI BREWING** Brewer, Kirk Lombardi
	TAPS SPORTS BAR AND GRILL Chef, Scott "Manno" Manning

GERMAN PRETZEL STICKS

PREP TIME: Active 20-30 minutes. Waiting 1½ hours
24 SERVINGS

½	cup water	1	teaspoon salt
1	teaspoon sugar	3½	cups all-purpose flour
1	package active dry yeast	4	tablespoons baking soda
¾	cup milk	1	egg, beaten
4	teaspoons olive oil		course salt

Using a large mixing bowl, or a mixer with dough hook, dissolve sugar in water. Stir in yeast, and let stand about five to 10 minutes, until bubbly. Mix together milk and oil, then add to bowl. Add salt and three cups all-purpose flour and mix. Add more flour as needed until ball forms. Let dough hook knead ball for a few minutes. Let dough rise about 30-60 minutes, covered, in a warm, draft-free area, until about double in size. In the meantime, prepare "soda bath." Put two quarts of water in pot and add four tablespoons baking soda. Mix. Bring to boil and keep hot until needed.

Preheat oven to 425°. Cover two baking sheets with parchment paper. Divide dough in half, and then each half into 12 pieces. Roll each piece into a stick about 5 inches long. Place pretzels onto baking sheets. Cover and let rise about 10 minutes. Gently place pretzels into boiling soda water, without crowding. When they rise to the surface, remove with slotted spoon and place back on baking sheets. Snip slits into tops with scissors. Gently brush egg wash over each stick. Sprinkle with coarse salt. Bake about 15 minutes until golden brown. Place on a rack to cool.

ZWEI DUNKEL BEER MUSTARD

PREP TIME: Active 10 minutes, waiting 2 days
YIELDS 12 OUNCES

½	cup apple cider vinegar	¼	cup Zwei Dunkel
¼	cup yellow mustard seeds	2	teaspoons brown sugar
¼	cup brown mustard seeds	1	teaspoon salt

Combine vinegar, beer and mustard seeds in small bowl, cover and let sit at room temperature for two days. Use food processor to blend soaked mustard seeds with salt and sugar until almost puréed. Put into appropriate container and refrigerate for up to two months.

CHEF'S NOTE: I enjoy this pretzel and mustard combination almost daily and believe me, it pairs great with Zwei's Dunkel!

BREWER'S PAIRING: Zwei Dunkel Lager
Beer + Pretzel = No Brainer.

"WE HAVE SO MUCH FUN WITH THE SMOKER—I CAN'T GET ENOUGH. I LOVE EXPERIMENTING WITH SMOKED BLUE CHEESE, ALMONDS, SALMON AND PULLED PORK. WE HAVE SOME DARN GOOD BBQ!"

- SCOTT "MANNO" MANNING

SPICY BRAISED PULLED PORK

COLLABORATION	**ZWEI BREWING** Brewer, Kirk Lombardi
	TAPS SPORTS BAR AND GRILL Chef, Scott "Manno" Manning

PREP TIME: 30 minutes
TOTAL TIME: 4 hours
8 SERVINGS

4-4½	pound boneless pork butt (remove netting or twine)		6	medium garlic cloves, smashed
2	tablespoons kosher salt		6	chipotle peppers in adobo, chopped
1	tablespoon black pepper		2	medium yellow onions, halved and thinly sliced
1	tablespoon ground chili powder		24	ounces Zwei Dunkel (or a brown ale of your choice)
½	teaspoon ground cinnamon			
1	tablespoon yellow mustard			
2	tablespoons vegetable oil			

1 Heat the oven to 300° and arrange a rack in the middle. Place salt, chili powder, and cinnamon in a small bowl and stir to combine. Coat pork butt with one tablespoon of mustard, and then coat all sides with the spice mixture. Let sit at room temperature for 30 minutes.

2 Heat two tablespoons oil over medium-high heat in a Dutch oven or a large, heavy-bottomed pot with a tight fitting lid until just starting to smoke (about three minutes). Add pork, and brown on all sides (about 15 minutes total). Remove pork to a plate and discard all but one tablespoon of the fat in the pot.

3 Reduce heat to medium and add garlic, peppers, and onions. Cook, scraping up any browned bits from the bottom of the pot, until softened (about 15 minutes). Increase heat to medium high, deglaze pan with beer, return pork to pan and bring to a boil. Cover, transfer to the oven, cook until pork is 195° internal temperature, and tender and falls apart when shredded with a fork (about three hours).

4 Allow pork to rest for 20-30 minutes. Remove pork to baking dish and use two forks to pull pork into shreds. Remove any large chunks of fat and add braising liquid and vegetables until you reach a nice moist texture.

CHEF'S NOTE: I will use this in a variety of ways, in burritos or tacos or just placed on a nice fresh brioche roll. Enjoy!

BREWER'S PAIRING: Zwei IPA
The sweet citrus notes of the IPA pair well with the sweetness of the sauce, while the hop bitterness adds contrasts.

BEER BRAISED CORNED BEEF HASH & EGGS

COLLABORATION | **ZWEI BREWING** Brewer, Kirk Lombardi | **SILVER GRILL CAFÉ** Chef, Heather Beckman

BEER BRAISED CORNED BEEF

(cook a day in advance)
PREP TIME: 10 minutes
COOK TIME: 5 hours
6 SERVINGS

5-7	pounds corned beef brisket (raw and pre-seasoned)	1	onion, quartered, skin and all
2	carrots (don't peel)	6	garlic cloves (whole, don't peel)
2	celery stalks	1	quart of Zwei Weissbier

Do not trim the corned beef or rinse the meat (you want all that spicy goodness). Just drain well. Pre-heat oven to 325°. In a Dutch oven, or any deep oven proof pan that will fit the whole piece of corned beef, place quartered onions, celery stalks, carrots and garlic cloves in the bottom of the pan. Top with whole piece of corned beef; add beer, and enough water to cover completely. Cover with lid or aluminum foil and bake for five hours. After five hours remove from braising liquid and cool completely (overnight).

BEER BRAISED CORNED BEEF HASH & EGGS

PREP TIME: 40 minutes
COOK TIME: 20 minutes
6 SERVINGS

5-7	pounds cooled corned beef brisket, ground or finely diced (see beer braised corned beef recipe)	2	ounces butter
		6	garlic cloves, minced
3	boiled and cooled whole potatoes for frying with hash	2	teaspoons salt
		2	teaspoons pepper
1	green pepper, small diced	12	eggs

Cook and cool three average sized potatoes for slicing, frying and mixing with corned beef hash.

Cook onions, peppers, garlic and butter in skillet. Add salt and pepper to season. Cook for 10 minutes or until translucent. Cool completely.

Lightly trim fat off corned beef, leaving some for frying and flavor. If you have a meat grinder, grind corned beef. If not, dice very finely into very small cubes.

Combine the corned beef with the onions and pepper mixture.

CHEF'S NOTE: For family style, in a large deep skillet, cook the sliced potatoes in 2 tablespoons of butter until golden brown and crispy. Add combined hash and cook until everything is warm and crispy. Add eggs to top of dish for service.

BREWER'S NOTE: Zwei Weissbier
Traditionally the Zwei Weissbier is a great breakfast or lunch beer—so it's got that going for it. The light acidity and fruitiness of the Weissbier counters the oils of the corned beef hash and the viscosity of the egg yolks.

BACON AND BEER BRAISED CABBAGE

COLLABORATION | **ZWEI BREWING** Brewer, Kirk Lombardi   **SILVER GRILL CAFÉ** Chef, Heath

PREP TIME: 10 minutes
COOK TIME: 50 minutes
6 SERVINGS

2	tablespoons olive oil		1	large head of cabbage, cored and thinly sliced or shredded
12	slices of bacon		1	pint of Zwei Brewing Pils Beer
4-6	garlic cloves, minced		½	cup malt vinegar
1	large onion, sliced			
2	bay leaves			
1	tablespoon salt			
1	tablespoon pepper			
¼	cup brown sugar			

In a large pot, add the oil and cook the bacon until browned and crispy. Add the onion, garlic, bay leaves, salt and pepper. Add the cabbage, brown sugar, beer, and malt vinegar, stirring to mix. Reduce heat to low and simmer for about one hour.

CHEF'S NOTE: Any time of year, this dish is one of my favorites. Beers, bacon, braising—need I say more? Oh yeah! Cabbage! Some of my favorite things all in one amazing dish!

BREWER'S PAIRING: Zwei Weissbier

I would put the Zwei Weissbier with this dish. The spiciness of the Weissbeir pairs well with the sweetness of the braised cabbage.

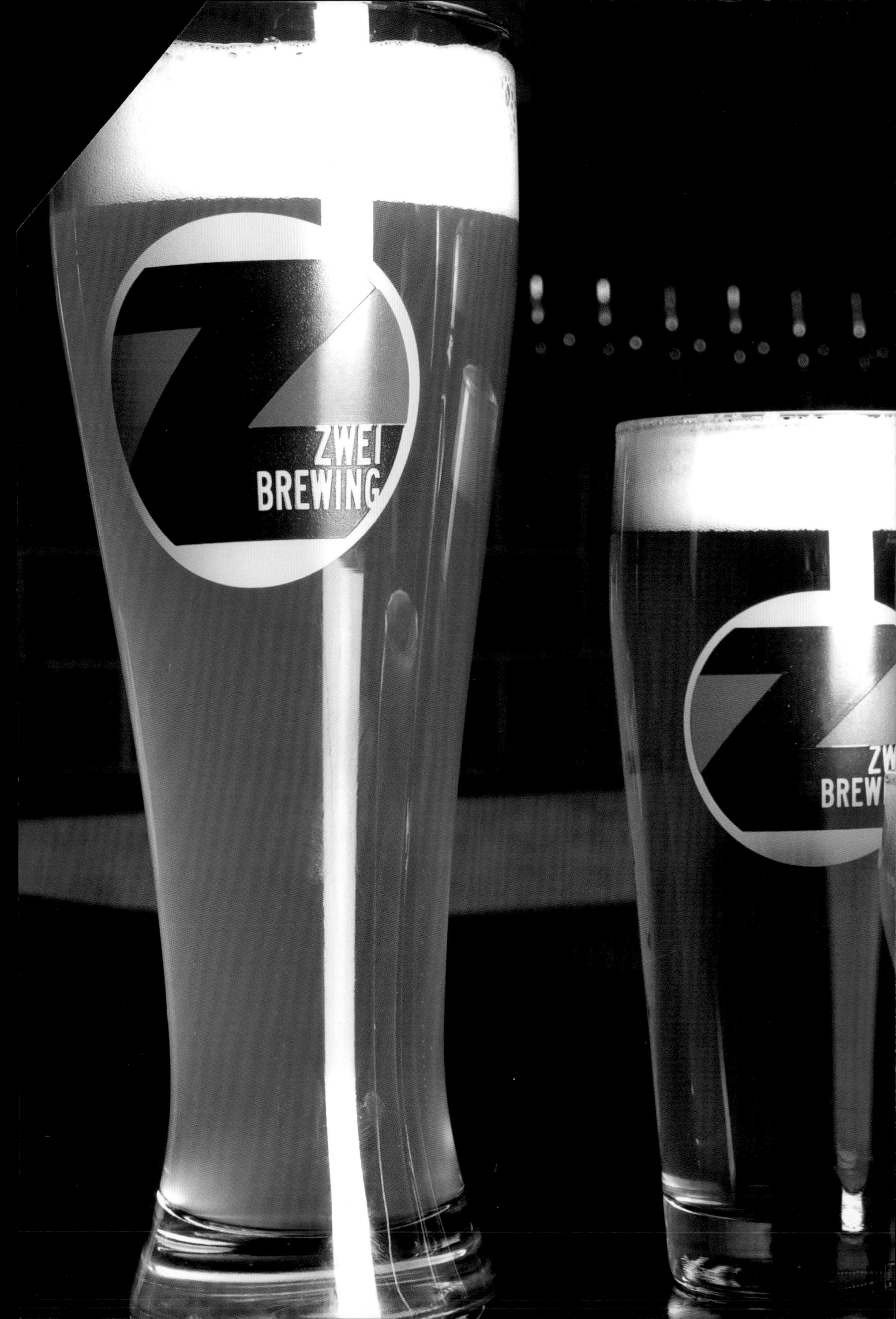
ZWEI
BREWING

BEER GLAZED SUGAR COOKIES

| COLLABORATION | **ZWEI BRWEING** Brewer, Kirk Lombardi |
| | **MARY'S MOUNTAIN COOKIES** Cookie Master, Mike Neal |

PREP TIME: 1 hour
YIELDS 40 SMALL COOKIES

SUGAR COOKIE:
4 sticks margarine

1 cup white sugar

2 eggs

3 teaspoons vanilla extract

12 teaspoons evaporated milk

2½ cups flour

3 teaspoons baking powder

1 teaspoon salt

BEER GLAZE:
1½ cups powdered sugar

1 teaspoon vanilla extract

2 cups Zwei Brewing Dunkelweizen

Mix margarine and white sugar on high speed until fluffy. Then add egg, vanilla extract, and evaporated milk on low speed for 30 seconds. Finally add flour, baking powder, and salt on low speed until dough is completely mixed. Heat oven to 325°. Spoon onto pan and bake for about 10 minutes. To be a master baker you must understand that baking times vary from oven to oven. It's better to start with a lesser time and add one or two minutes. Ask yourself, do you like your cookies soft or crispy? For the glaze, simply mix all ingredients on high speed. Dunk the cooled cookies into the glaze and there you have it—Beer Glazed Sugar Cookies.

CHEF'S NOTE: Making the perfect dough takes time. Write your times and speeds down and adjust for the next batch. Cookies flat? Beat those sugars until super fluffy!

BREWER'S PAIRING: Zwei Dunkelweizen
This Bavarian dark wheat beer pairs well with Mary's short bread cookie. The simplicity of the short bread cookie complements the chocolate and banana notes of the beer without overwhelming it. The lingering sweetness and hint of nutmeg and clove in the beer, along with the bready splendor of the short bread leaves the taster in complete beer and cookie bliss.

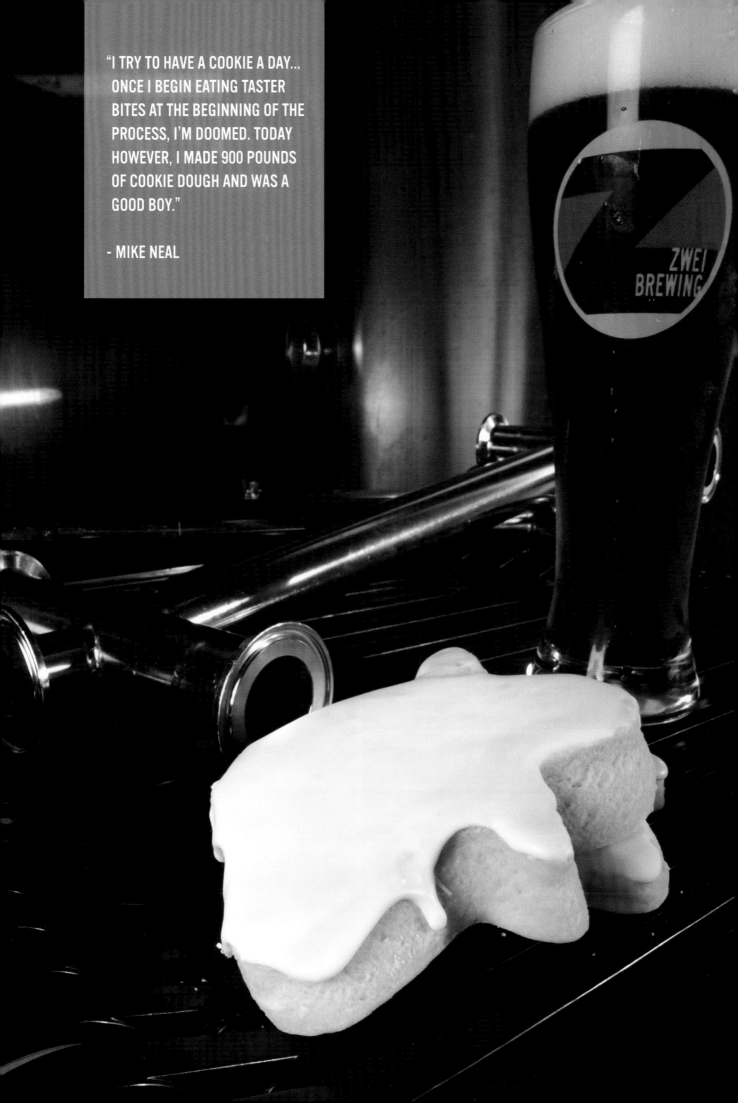

"I TRY TO HAVE A COOKIE A DAY...
ONCE I BEGIN EATING TASTER
BITES AT THE BEGINNING OF THE
PROCESS, I'M DOOMED. TODAY
HOWEVER, I MADE 900 POUNDS
OF COOKIE DOUGH AND WAS A
GOOD BOY."

- MIKE NEAL

INDEX